THE Ol

SNOWBIRD'S

GUIDE

TO BECOMING

A FLORIDA RESIDENT

Dean Hanewinckel

Dean Biz, Inc.

ISBN-13: 978-0-9818233-0-0
ISBN-10: 0-9818233-0-0

Library of Congress Control Number: 2008908259

Subject Headings:
Florida
Florida reference
Travel
 Florida travel

CONTENTS

INTRODUCTION

It's Great to Live In Florida

As I write, I am finishing lunch on the patio of the Pink Elephant Eating and Drinking Establishment in the little island village of Boca Grande. A light, warm breeze drifts in from the Gulf of Mexico, barely ruffling the umbrella that shields me from the bright Florida sunshine. Less than a hundred feet in front of me, a fabulous yacht is moored, complete with a helicopter in the event its owner needs to get someplace quickly. That's not likely. Nothing happens quickly on the island. A couple of hundred yards to my left is the private Gasparilla Inn golf course, played by captains of industry, movie stars and U.S. Presidents. About three miles to my right is Boca Grande Pass, home, according to the locals, of the "World's Greatest Tarpon Fishing."I take the last bite of my grilled grouper and think to myself, "It's great to live in Florida."

Apparently, I'm not the only one with that thought. Each year over 300,000 people become new residents of Florida. Some of these residents find their way to my law office seeking answers and advice about moving to Florida.

It was from these clients and their inquiries that I realized that there was no resource where someone could get all their questions answered about becoming a Florida resident. I undertook the challenge to put together such a resource.

A resource that would not just address the steps necessary to achieve residency (although that is covered in this book); but would explain how your estate plan is affected and how to purchase or build a home in Florida. A resource that would clearly and completely explain Florida homestead and how you can minimize your property taxes and protect your assets with it. A resource that would help you acquire a driver's license, a fishing license and qualify for in-state college tuition. The *complete* guide to becoming a Florida resident.

If you need more information than this book is able to provide, I've made a companion website available to you. Visit www.newfloridaresident.com and you will have access to information, forms and links to Florida agencies and organizations all in one place. The resources will make it easy to move to Florida. Your toughest assignment will be to find your own perfect piece of paradise.

CHAPTER 1

Becoming A Florida Resident

After spending the winters, or even longer, in Florida, you realize that becoming a Florida resident would be the thing for you. Florida has a reputation of being a tax-friendly state for its residents. There is no state income tax and gift and estate taxation is less of a burden than most states.

Florida is a great place to protect your assets from the claims of creditors. Just ask a certain former hall of fame football player who likes to play golf. Florida laws provide creditor protection for your homestead, your annuities and the cash value of your life insurance policies.

While property taxes have recently gone up, residents can enjoy lower taxes on their homestead through exemptions and the "Save Our Homes" cap on property tax increases.

Combine that with the weather, the beaches, the fishing and golf and it becomes almost impossible to resist becoming a Floridian.

In Florida, the courts have ruled that your legal residence is determined by your intention. Therefore, if you come to Florida with the intention of making this state your primary residence then you are a Florida resident and are entitled to the advantages and privileges that go along with it. Sounds easy doesn't it?

However, in many cases it is difficult to determine exactly what a person's intentions are. That's why it's important to provide clear evidence of your intention to become a Florida resident. In this chapter you will learn the procedure necessary to prove your intention to establish residency and the small details that will help to convince your former state of residence that you no longer reside there.

Once you make the decision to become a Florida resident, you should make sure that everything about you shows that you are a Floridian. For example: a Florida resident is not registered to vote in Massachusetts; a Florida resident does not carry a Michigan drivers license; a Florida resident does not own or drive around in a car registered in Ohio; and a Florida resident does not root for the Yankees. O.K., maybe you can get by with that last one.

Before establishing residency in Florida, you should review the laws of your previous state to see what you will have to do to terminate residency in that state. If you comply with those requirements and adhere to the following procedures, then you will provide solid evidence of your intent to be a resident of Florida.

File a Declaration of Domicile. Upon making Florida your permanent residence, the first thing you should do is file a Declaration of Domicile in the Clerk of Circuit Court's office. This document is a sworn statement that you reside in and maintain a place of residence in the Florida county where you live and that you intend to maintain that residence as your permanent home. If you also have a residence or residences in other states, you may disclose them and declare that your Florida residence is your primary home.

The Declaration of Domicile form is available from the office of the Clerk of Circuit Court. You can either visit the Clerk's office or obtain the form online. You should fill in the information requested on the form and sign it. Your signature must be acknowledged by a notary public. It should then be recorded in the public records of the county of your residence. This can be done by paying the Clerk a small fee. Many people also send a copy to the tax authorities of their former state of residence as evidence that they are now Florida residents and do not reside in that state.

Apply for the Homestead Exemption. If as of January 1, you (1) are a Florida resident, (2) have legal and equitable ownership to your home and (3) have established it as your permanent residence, you are eligible for obtaining the homestead exemption. You must file an application for Homestead Exemption at the Property Appraisers Office in the county where you live on or before March 1st of the year in which you seek application.

When making the application, you must bring the following documents:

1.   a Florida drivers license, Florida identification card or Declaration of Domicile showing that you were a Florida resident on or before January 1.

2.   a Florida vehicle registration for all automobiles owned by you.

3.   a Florida voter registration card in the county where you are applying (if you are registered to vote)

4.   Social Security Number of each owner/applicant

5.   a copy of your recorded deed or a tax bill to show you own the property. It must be dated on or before January 1.

The normal filing time for homestead exemption begins on January 1 and continues through March 1. You must file the application for that year by March 1 or you will have to wait until the next year to get the exemption. You may prefile for the following year in most counties from March 2 through December 31. I would recommend that you do this in order to avoid lines and to begin the "Save Our Homes" cap on property tax increases a year earlier than if you applied after the first of the year.

We'll talk about the "Save Our Homes" cap and the other benefits of the homestead exemption later in the Chapter on Florida Homestead

<u>Obtain a Florida Driver's License</u>. Florida law requires that you obtain a Florida driver's license within 30 days after becoming a resident of Florida. To obtain a Florida driver's license, you must present a form of identification, proof of your date of birth and your social security number. United States citizens must submit one of the following primary documents:

1.   Original or certified copy of your United States birth certificate, or

2.   Valid United States passport, or

3.   Certificate of Naturalization.

You must also provide one of the following secondary documents:

- Social Security Card

- Florida voter registration card or a Florida or out-of-state driver's license, valid or expired
- School record stating date of birth, which must contain the registrar's signature
- Baptism certificate (showing date of birth and place of baptism)
- An insurance policy on your life which has been in force for at least two years and contains your date of birth; marriage certificate.

Depending on which state you are from, you may be able to use your former state's driver's license as a primary identification document. If you have an out-of-state license and it has not expired beyond 30 days, you may be able to convert it to a Florida license without taking a written or road test. Canadian citizens may be issued a Florida driver's license by presenting 2 of the following documents:

- Canadian passport
- Canadian driver's license
- Original or certified copy of a Canadian birth certificate.

Re-Title and Register Your Cars. You must apply for a Florida certificate of title for any vehicle you own and operate in the state of Florida. Your vehicle must be registered within ten days of establishing residency. To register your vehicle, submit the original title and proof of Florida insurance to the county tax collector. If you are registering the vehicle in Florida for the first time, you'll have to pay a $100 initial registration fee in addition to the basic registration fees. You are required to register your car every year. The registration period begins the first day of your birth month and ends on your birthday the next year.

Register to Vote. One of the best ways to show your intention to be a Florida resident is to register to vote in your county and participate in local, state and federal elections as a Florida voter. You may register with the county Supervisor of Elections when the voter registration books are open. The books close 30 days before an election and reopen following the election. Also, in most counties, selection for jury duty is taken from the roll of registered voters.

Change Your Will. You should have a Will prepared by a Florida attorney that complies with Florida law and says that you are a resident of Florida. This new Will revokes your prior Will and makes sure that your estate is distributed according to your wishes with the least amount of complications and delay. If you have a revocable trust, it should be reviewed by a Florida attorney to determine whether its terms comply with Florida law and whether it will be interpreted under Florida law the way you want. Most out-of-state trusts will have to be amended to address the Florida homestead law.

If you look at your current Will, it will likely say (usually in the first paragraph) that you are a resident of your prior state. Some states take that declaration very seriously. They reason that a Florida resident wouldn't have a Will that states he is a resident of Pennsylvania.

This was the ruling in a 1992 case in the Pennsylvania Commonwealth Court. The court ruled that a person who died in Florida was a Pennsylvania resident and subject to Pennsylvania tax, despite the fact that he received a Florida homestead exemption, had a Florida vehicle registration and driver's license, had bank accounts in Florida, filed his federal income taxes with a Florida address and spent eight months of each year in Florida. The court stated that its decision was based largely on the declaration in his Will that he was a Pennsylvania resident.

Change your Will.

File Your Taxes Like a Floridian. Federal income tax returns should be filed in Atlanta, Georgia. As a Florida resident, you must also file Florida tangible tax return, if applicable. I have to assume that you don't want to pay any more taxes to your former state than you absolutely have to. If you still own property in your previous state, they will probably still want some of your tax money. Don't give them more than they are entitled to. File only those tax returns in your former state that are required for non-residents.

Change Your Memberships and Affiliations. You should cancel your memberships in and affiliations with churches, organizations and clubs in your previous state of residence or transfer them to Florida.

Other items that can be used to show your intent to make Florida your primary place of residence include:

- Location of your bank accounts, safe deposit boxes and securities.
- Children's school attendance
- Business interests and activities
- Percentage of time spent in each state

Statutory Residency Requirements.

Florida has a number of statutes that address the requirements for being considered a Florida resident for specific purposes.

The Declaration of Domicile that we discussed earlier in this Chapter is authorized by Florida law. **Section 222.17** of the Florida Statutes states in part that "Any person who shall have established a domicile in this state may manifest and evidence the same by filing in the office of the clerk of the circuit court for the county in which the said person shall reside, a sworn statement showing that he or she resides in and maintains a place of abode in that county which he or she recognizes and intends to maintain as his or her permanent home." It further states that a person wishing to establish residency in Florida that maintains a home in another state "may manifest and evidence his or her domicile in this state by filing in the office of the clerk of the circuit court for the county in which he or she resides, a sworn statement that his or her place of abode in Florida constitutes his or her predominant and principal home, and that he or she intends to continue it permanently as such."

Section 196.015 lists a number of factors the county property appraiser may consider in determining whether a person is a Florida resident for property tax and homestead reasons. The statute reads as follows:

196.015. Permanent residency; factual determination by property appraiser.--Intention to establish a permanent residence in this state is a factual determination to be made, in the first instance, by the property appraiser. Although any one factor is not conclusive of the establishment or nonestablishment of permanent residence, the following are relevant factors that may be considered by the property appraiser in making his or her determination as to the intent of a person claiming a homestead exemption to establish a permanent residence in this state:

(1) Formal declarations of the applicant.

(2) Informal statements of the applicant.

(3) The place of employment of the applicant.

(4) The previous permanent residency by the applicant in a state other than Florida or in another country and the date non-Florida residency was terminated.

(5) The place where the applicant is registered to vote.

(6) The place of issuance of a driver's license to the applicant.

(7) The place of issuance of a license tag on any motor vehicle owned by the applicant.

(8) The address as listed on federal income tax returns filed by the applicant.

(9) The previous filing of Florida intangible tax returns by the applicant.

Florida Statute 1009.21 requires that for in-state tuition purposes, a person or, if that person is a dependent child, his or her parent or parents must have established legal residence in this state and must have maintained legal residence in this state for at least 12 months immediately prior to his or her qualification. You will read more about this in Chapter 11.

Here are some other suggestions to show your Florida residency:

(1) List your Florida residence as the primary residence on all homeowners insurance policies.

(2) Obtain a Florida library card and get rid of your old one. Especially if it is only available to residents of your former state.

(3) Move your professional relationships such as attorneys, accountants, financial advisors and doctors to those practicing in Florida.

(4) Don't take advantage of benefits available only to residents of your previous state.

Welcome to Florida. Now that you know what to do, get to work.

CHAPTER 2

Taxes In Florida

Here in Florida, we don't have any state income tax. But you knew that already, didn't you? Florida and its counties raise their revenue mainly with a combination of sales taxes, property taxes and transfer taxes. You used to have to pay an intangible tax on your investments, but that tax was repealed in 2007. The tax that you will notice the most will be your property taxes. Property taxes are divided into two groups: real estate taxes and personal property taxes.

Real Estate Taxes. If you own real estate in Florida, whether you are a resident or not, you must pay taxes on your property. Each November your county will send you a property tax bill. When you look at your tax bill you are going to see two categories: ad valorem and non- ad valorem.

Ad Valorem Taxes. Ad valorem real estate taxes are taxes based on the value of the property. The County Property Appraiser establishes the value of each parcel of real property in the county. Taxing authorities, such as the Board of County Commissioners, school board, water management board, and others set the millage rates. A millage rate is the rate of tax per one thousand dollars of the taxable value of your property. Each taxing authority has a different millage rate. The millage rate for general county operations and maintenance is set by the Board of County Commissioners. In addition, various other taxing authorities, such as school boards, set their own millage rates. To determine the ad valorem tax on a property, you must divide the taxable value of your property by 1,000 and multiply that result by the total of all millage rates. For example, if the taxable value of your property is $300,000 and your county's school board has set a millage rate of 4.5000, the ad valorem tax attributed to the School Board would be $1,350.00. You would then add together all of the tax from each taxing authority to determine your total ad valorem tax amount.

Don't worry, you won't have to figure it out. The County Tax Collector is kind enough to do all the calculations for you. All you have to do is write the check.

What is the Taxable Value of Your Property? Each year your county's Property Appraiser's office is required to determine the assessed value of every piece of property in the county. The Property Appraiser determines the "Just" or "Fair Market Value" of your property. This is what he believes your property would sell for in an open market under normal conditions. He then subtracts the typical costs incurred in a sale of your property to arrive at the Assessed Value.

The Appraiser adjusts his opinion of the Market Value of your property each year based on many factors. An increase in the property values in the area will cause your Market Value to increase. If you add on to your house, it will likely increase. Conversely, unrepaired fire or hurricane damage, or a decrease in the area's economy will cause your Market Value to decrease.

The Assessed Value of the property is then reduced by any property tax exemptions for which you may qualify. The most well known of these is the homestead exemption. The first $25,000 and the $25,000 between $50,000 and $75,000 of the assessed value is exempt from taxes. This is one of the reasons why it is important that you apply for the homestead exemption as soon as possible.

The homestead property tax exemption and the "Save Our Homes Amendment" applicable to homestead property is discussed in detail in Chapter 3 of this book. In addition, there are other exemptions that may reduce the value of your home for property tax purposes.

$500 Widow's and Widower's Exemption. This exemption is available to Florida residents who are a widow or widower prior to January 1 of the tax year for which you are applying. Divorced persons do not qualify for this exemption and a widow or widower becomes ineligible upon remarriage.

Veteran Disability Exemption. A $5,000 Veteran disability exemption is available to veterans and the unremarried widow or widower of a disabled veteran. The veteran must provide proof issued by the U.S. Veterans Administration of 10% or more permanent service related disability. The surviving spouse of a disabled veteran must have been married to the veteran for at least five years at the time of the veteran's death. This exemption is applicable to any property owned by the veteran.

$500 Disability Exemption. A Florida resident may apply for this exemption if he or she can show proof of either (1) total and permanent disability (from 2 unrelated licensed Florida physicians or the U.S. Veterans Administration) or (2) legal blindness, or (3) ten percent or more war-time disability from the Veterans Administration.

Total Exemption of Homestead. Homestead real estate owned by quadriplegic, paraplegic, hemiplegic, or other totally and permanently disabled persons, who must use a wheelchair for mobility, or are legally blind, is exempt from ad valorem taxation. A person seeking this exemption who is not a quadriplegic or veteran, must meet certain gross income limitations. For this purpose gross income includes veteran's and social security benefits and includes the gross income of all persons residing in the homestead for the prior year. The gross income limitations are adjusted annually. You should ask your county Property Appraiser's office to obtain these limitation amounts.

Additional Homestead Exemption for Persons 65 and Over. The Florida Constitution provides that a county or a municipality may adopt an ordinance to allow an additional $25,000 homestead exemption for persons 65 years of age or older. In order to receive the additional exemption, the following circumstances must be met:

1. The county or municipality must adopt an ordinance that allows the additional homestead exemption. If adopted this exemption applies **only** to the taxes levied by the unit of government granting the exemption. Check with your county's Property Appraiser's office to see if it offers this additional homestead exemption.

2. The owner of the property must by 65 years of age or older on January 1 of the year for which the exemption is claimed.

3. The annual household income of the owner (defined as the gross adjusted income of all members of the household) must not exceed $23,463 for the 2006 tax year. The income limitation is adjusted annually each January 1, based on the cost of living index.

Payment of Ad Valorem Taxes. You pay your ad valorem taxes in arrears. They are based on the calendar year from January 1 to December 31. Tax bills are mailed to you on November 1 of each year. This means that the tax bill you receive in November, 2008 will cover property taxes for the period beginning January 1, 2008 and ending December 31, 2008. If you have a mortgage on the property and your property taxes are paid from an escrow account established by the lender, the bill will usually be sent to the mortgage company and you will receive an informational notice.

Discounts for Paying Early. If the tax is paid during the month of November, you will receive a 4% discount. You get a 3% discount for paying in December, a 2% discount in January, and a

1% discount in February. The full tax is due in March. Taxes become delinquent on April 1.

Non Ad Valorem Assessments. Also included on your tax bill are assessments that are not based on the value of the property. These non ad valorem assessments are levied by authorities such as stormwater utility, fire and rescue, solid waste collections and sewer utilities in set amounts.

Installment Payment Plan. You have an option to pay your real estate taxes quarterly. You must fill out and return an Installment Plan application form to the Tax Collector's Office prior to May 1.

Delinquent Taxes. If you have not paid the property taxes by April 1, the Tax Collector is required by law to advertise your delinquent property in a local newspaper once a week for three consecutive weeks. All fees for advertising and collection are added to your tax bill.

By June 1, the Tax Collector will hold a tax certificate sale. At this sale, your tax bill will come up for auction. Anyone wanting to participate can bid on your tax certificate. But this isn't a typical auction. The participants are not bidding money. The amount the winner will pay has already been set. The winning bidder will pay the total amount of your tax bill. What they are bidding on is the interest rate they will earn if you wish to redeem your tax certificate. The bidding begins at 18% and continues downward. The certificate is awarded to the bidder who pays the taxes due and is willing to accept the lowest interest rate. The certificate is a lien against your property securing the amount of delinquent taxes plus accrued interest (at the bid for rate), penalties and advertising fees. If you redeem your Certificate, the Tax Collector pays the certificate holder the amount due to him or her.

Why would you want to redeem the certificate? Because after 2 years the certificate holder may apply for a tax deed. If you fail to pay the tax debt, the tax deed is sold at public auction and you lose your property.

Tangible Personal Property Tax. If you own a rental property or some other type of income producing property you are subject to the tangible personal property tax. Tangible personal property tax is an ad valorem tax assessed against the furniture, fixtures and equipment located in businesses and rental property. The County Property Appraiser is responsible for assessing the value of the tangible personal property. The value is based on a personal property inventory return that you are required to file each year.

The amount of the tax due is calculated by multiplying the value of the property by the tax rate set by the taxing authorities.

The tangible personal property tax bills are mailed on November 1, and the same discounts for early payment apply. On or before April 1 of the next year Tax Warrants are issued for all unpaid taxes. The Tax Collector may apply to Circuit Court for an order directing seizure of the property to pay the unpaid amounts.

Sales Tax. The state of Florida acquires most of its revenue from a six percent tax on each sale, admission charge, storage or rental that is not specifically exempt. The sales tax is added to the price of taxable goods and services and collected from the purchaser at the time of sale. For example, if you purchase an item costing $100.00, you will pay a 6% state sales tax in addition to the sales price at the time of payment. The total amount you would pay for the transaction is $106.00.

Some examples of items that you would be required to pay a sales tax on are new and used retail goods, restaurant meals, rent or lease of commercial property, rent or lease of living accommodations for a period of six months or less (including hotels, houses and condominiums), admission to sports events, performances and amusement parks, and certain services.

In addition to the state sales tax, Florida counties are authorized to levy a discretionary sales surtax. The rate of the discretionary sales surtax varies depending on the county. In fact, not all counties levy this tax.

Sales Tax Holiday. On a year by year basis, the Florida legislature has offered a sales tax holiday for a week shortly before the start of the school year. The holiday provides for a sales tax exemption for each eligible book or clothing item selling for $50.00 or less and certain school supplies having a sales price of $10.00 or less.

Use Tax. The Florida use tax applies to purchases of taxable goods or services that are brought into Florida within six months of the purchase date and have not previously been taxed or have been taxed at a rate less than the Florida sales tax rate. These taxes usually apply to goods purchased over the internet or a mail-order catalog service. The tax is intended to provide uniform taxation on items that are purchased outside of Florida but are used or stored in the state.

Tourist Development Tax. Some counties levy tourist development taxes on transient rental transactions (rentals or leases in hotels, motels, apartments, rooming houses, trailers, camps, mobile homes or condominiums for a period of six months or less). This tax is commonly referred to as the "bed tax." Rates vary according to county, but may not exceed six percent. The revenues are generally used for construction of tourist related facilities, tourism promotion and beach renourishment.

Documentary Stamp Tax. The state of Florida levies a Documentary Stamp Tax on the transfer of real estate in the state. You may have noticed this listed on the settlement statement when you purchased your Florida property. The tax rate is $0.70 per $100.00 of the total purchase price. For typical transfers of real estate in Florida, one of the larger expenses of the transaction is the documentary stamp tax on the deed. For example, if a home in Florida is sold for $500,000.00, the documentary stamp tax on the transaction would be $3,500.00 ($500,000.00 / $100 X .70)

In Miami-Dade County there is a lesser rate of $0.60 per $100.00 (or portion thereof) when the property is a single-family residence. If the Miami-Dade County property is not a single-family residence, the tax rate is $0.60 plus $0.45 surtax per $100.00.

The state also imposes a Documentary Stamp Tax on all written obligations to pay money. These include promissory notes, retail installment sales contracts, and title loans. The rate of the tax is $0.35 for each $100.00.

Intangible Tax. Prior to January 1, 2007, Florida was one of only four states that imposed a tax on intangible personal property. The state levied an annual tax based on the current market value, as of January 1, of a Florida resident's intangible personal property such as stocks, bonds, mutual funds and other investment property.

The intangible personal property tax was repealed effective January 1, 2007.

Not affected by the repeal is a non-recurring intangible tax due on mortgages and documents secured by Florida real estate. The tax rate is 2 mills (.002) per dollar (the tax on a $100,000 mortgage would be $200.00) and is payable at the time of recording the mortgage or other document. If you finance the purchase of real estate with a mortgage loan, you will pay an intangible tax based on the amount of the mortgage in addition to the documentary stamp tax on the promissory note.

Florida Estate Tax. Even though Florida has no inheritance tax, it does have an estate tax. This is a tax based on the size of your estate at the time of death. For purposes of estate tax, your estate consists of all property that you own, totally or partially, at the time of your death, whether such property is subject to probate, is jointly owned, is held by your revocable trust or is disposed of by beneficiary designations.

Florida's estate tax is known as a "pick up tax," which means that it absorbs or "picks up" the federal estate tax credit for state death taxes.

If an estate is not required to file a federal estate tax return (IRS Form 706), then no Florida estate tax is due. In 2008, an estate is required to file a Form 706 if the size of your gross estate exceeds $2,000,000. In 2009, that threshold will be $3,500,000.

The Florida estate tax system is designed such that the estate of a Florida resident owning only Florida property will not have to pay more than the total amount due to the federal government if there were not state tax credits. If a Florida resident owned real estate in a state other than Florida, he may owe an estate tax to that state.

The filing of the estate tax return on the payment of the Florida estate tax is due nine months after the date of death.

Obtaining a Release of the Florida Estate Tax Lien. If a personal representative of a decedent's estate, a trustee of a decedent's trust or a successor owner to a decedent wishes to sell real property owned by the decedent at the time of his death, the potential or actual lien for the estate taxes must be released to clear title to the property.

If a decedent's estate is not large enough to require filing of a Federal Estate Tax Return (Form 706), then the personal representative must file an affidavit of No Florida Estate Tax Due (Florida Department of Revenue Form DR-312) with the clerk in the decedent's county of residence and record it in the public records of every county where the decedent owned real property. This form is available online at the Florida Department of Revenue website.

If the decedent's estate is required to file a Federal Estate Tax Return (Form 706), the tax must be paid to the federal government and the State of Florida. The IRS reviews the 706 and if everything is proper, issues an Estate Tax Closing letter. The Florida Department of Revenue, upon receipt of the Estate Tax Closing letter and payment of Florida estate taxes, issues a Final Certificate. The Final Certificate is then recorded in the public records of each county where the decedent owned real property. This shows that there is no longer an estate tax lien affecting the property.

If the property must be sold prior to issuance of the Final Certificate, the personal representative may apply for a waiver of the Florida estate tax lien. She does this by filing a Request and Certificate for Waiver and Release of Florida Estate Tax Lien

(Florida Department of Revenue Form DR-308). If the estimated tax has been paid the Department of Revenue may issue a certificate of release of lien.

CHAPTER 3

Florida Homestead

One of the most advantageous yet confusing features of Florida residency is the homestead exemption. You've heard how you can greatly reduce your property tax by applying for the homestead tax exemption. However, the effects of homestead in Florida go a lot further.

There are actually three aspects to the Florida homestead law:

1) the tax exemption which reduces the taxable value of your real property by up to $50,000 and which includes the "Save Our Homes" Amendment,
2) the exemption from forced sale by creditors, and
3) the restrictions on transfer of homestead, both during your lifetime and after your death.

What Property Is Homestead? Before we tackle these three aspects, we need to determine what property qualifies for homestead treatment. Article X, Section 4 of the Florida Constitution defines homestead property as property owned by a natural person, "if located outside a municipality, to the extent of 160 acres of contiguous land and improvements thereon, ... or, if located within a municipality, to the extent of one-half acre of contiguous land, upon which the exemption shall be limited to the residence of the owner or the owner's family." Say what? O.K., let's break this down to come up with some standards to use to identify homestead property.

Must Be Owned By a Natural Person. This means that the property must be owned by an individual or individuals. Corporations, limited liability companies or other business entities cannot qualify for homestead exemption. If you wish to qualify for the homestead exemption, you cannot title your home in the name of a corporation (even if you are the only stockholder), a family limited partnership or other business entity. You may however own your home in a revocable trust, provided that you are the trustee of the trust and also a beneficiary of the trust and either you or your family resides on the property. The homestead can also be owned by a husband and wife as tenants by the entireties and in the form of a life estate.

How Large Can My Homestead Be? Your property must be located in Florida. If you live outside of a municipality (or city) the size of your property may not exceed 160 acres. If you live within a city's limits your homestead is limited to one-half acre. If you purchase a home of 160 acres outside a municipality and the property is later incorporated into a municipality, your homestead may not be reduced unless you consent.

Contiguous Land. This means that all parts of the homestead property must abut or be touching. If the parcel is divided by a state or county road, or by a body of water not owned by the owner of the homestead property, the parcel is not contiguous and only the part where the owner actually resides is considered to be homestead. An easement across the property, however, will not keep the parcel from being contiguous. If you later purchase a piece of land which is contiguous to your existing homestead, it may qualify for homestead status. For example, if you purchase the vacant lot next to your homestead, it will become a part of the homestead, provided it is contiguous to the original property and both properties together do not exceed the size limitations.

It Must Be Your Residence. You or your family must reside on the property for it to be considered your homestead. The definition of family in this instance may include more than the traditional family. Family, in this context, includes those who you are legally obligated to support, those who you actually support, and your spouse.

The qualifying resident must be a resident of Florida; however you need not be a United States citizen since citizenship is not necessary for permanent residency. The property must be your principal and permanent residence. You cannot treat the property in any other manner than as your permanent residence. For example, if you rent out your property for a portion of the year, it will no longer qualify as homestead property.

The Homestead Tax Exemption. The first benefit of being a resident of Florida and owning homestead property is the homestead tax exemption. Every county in Florida levies an ad valorem property tax on all real property in the county. This tax is calculated by multiplying the taxable value of the property (as determined by the county property appraiser) by the millage rate (as determined by the local taxing authorities such as the county commission, city council, school board and special taxing districts). The homestead exemption reduces the taxable value of your homestead property by $25,000, resulting in a reduction of ad valorem taxes on your home. In January, 2008, the citizens of Florida approved Amendment 1 to its state constitution and created an additional homestead exemption of $25,000 to lower the taxable value of homestead property for all taxes except those levied by school districts. The exemption applies on the assessed value of the homestead property that exceeds $50,000. This means that, if the just valuation of your homestead property is $100,000, the first $25,000 of value and the assessed value between $50,000 and $75,000 would be exempt from taxes. However, the value between $50,000 and $75,000 would still be used to determine the amount of school tax.

As an example, let's look at the taxes on a hypothetical piece of property, first without the homestead exemption and then with the exemption.

Without Homestead Exemption:

Assessed Value	$100,000
No Homestead Exemption	$ 0
Taxable Value	$100,000
Times Millage Rate (.010)*	
Times School Millage (.008)*	
Tax Due	$ 1,800

With Homestead Exemption:

Assessed Value	$100,000
Less Homestead Exemption	$ 50,000
Taxable Value (General Tax)	$ 50,000
Times Millage Rate (.010)*	
Tax Due	$ 500
Taxable Value (School Tax)	$ 75,000
Times School Millage (.008)**	
Tax Due	$ 600
Total Tax Due	$ 1,100

* The millage rate of .018 (18 Mills) has been arbitrarily chosen to illustrate the effect of homestead exemption. The rate will vary from county to county and from year to year.

** Additional homestead exemption does not apply to taxes levied by school
     districts

As you can see, the homestead exemption gave you a savings of $700 in the above example. The savings may be more or less depending on the millage rate set for that year in the county.

The "Save Our Homes" Amendment. Probably even more valuable than the homestead tax exemption is the "Save Our Homes" Amendment to the Florida Constitution. This amendment, passed in 1992 by the voters of Florida, limits the annual increase in the taxable value for homestead property to a maximum of 3% each year.

Each year, the county assesses the taxable value of all real property on its tax rolls. As a result of the amendment, the taxable value of property that qualifies for the homestead tax exemption may increase no more than 3 percent of the prior year's assessment or the percentage change in the Consumer Price Index, which ever is less. Of course, the taxable value can never exceed the just valuation (or market value) of the property.

The Market Value of your property increases based on the economic conditions and sales prices of other properties in your area. In some areas of Florida in the years between 2002 and 2006, the market value of some properties increased 20% or more each year for consecutive years. As a result, properties that were originally valued at $300,000 were worth almost $450,000 a couple of years later. You can imagine the increase in property taxes resulting from this.

However, if the $300,000 property was the owner's homestead, the increase in taxable value was limited to 3% per year. As a result, the taxable value of the property 2 years later would not be greater than $318,270, even though its Market Value was $450,000. This translates into a huge savings in property tax.

The amendment provides that after any change in ownership or any new qualification for homestead tax exemption, the homestead property shall be taxed at the just value as of January 1 of the year following the change in ownership. The amendments limits will apply each year following. So if you move to Florida, become a resident and qualify for homestead status, your property will be re-assessed on the first day of the year after you qualify for homestead at its just value with no limitations on the increase. Each year thereafter, the increase in taxable value will be limited by the amendment. For this reason, you should move into a new home and apply for the homestead exemption prior to the end of a calendar year so the initial reassessment takes place earlier. This causes the 3 percent cap to take effect a year earlier than if you waited until after the first of the year to apply.

Portability of the Save Our Homes Benefit. Under Save Our Homes, the assessed value of homestead property cannot increase more than 3% each year. Prior to the enactment of Amendment 1, if you sold your homestead and bought a new home, the taxable value of the new home would be equal to its Market Value. All of the benefits you accrued in your old home under the Save Our Homes amendment would be lost. As a result, some new homeowners suffered a large increase in property taxes even though the market value of the new home was not greater than that of the old one.

After January 1, 2008, under Amendment 1, you can transfer some of the Save Our Homes benefit to your new home.

If the market value of your new home is the same or greater than your old home's market value, the entire difference between market value and taxable value will be applied to your new home.

This is explained by the following illustration:

	Market Value	Taxable Value	Difference
Old Home	300,000	200,000	100,000
New Home	400,000	300,000	100,000

The market value of your old home at the time you sell it is $300,000. You have lived in it for 12 years and the taxable value at the time of sale is $200,000, creating a difference of $100,000. The market value of your new home at the time you purchased it is $400,000. Amendment 1 allows you to transfer the $100,000 difference from your old home and therefore the taxable value of your new home starts at $300,000. Prior to Amendment 1, the taxable value of the new home would have been equal to the market value: $400,000.

If the market value of your new home is less than that of your old home, you will not receive the entire difference. Instead, the new home's difference will be the same percentage of its market value as the old home's difference is of the old home's market value.

	Market Value	Taxable Value	Difference	% Difference
Old Home	300,000	200,000	100,000	33.3%
New Home	200,000	133,334	66,666	33.3%

In this example, the old home's Save Our Homes difference is 33.3% or 1/3 of its market value. The new home's difference would be 33.3% of its market value, or $66,666. Therefore, the taxable value of the new home would be $133,334.

Under Amendment 1, if you establish a new homestead and, (1) qualify for the homestead exemption by January 1 of a particular year and, (2) you had a homestead exemption on your old home in either of the two immediately preceding years and, (3) you apply for the homestead exemption and Amendment 1 transfer (of the difference) by March 1 of the particular year, then you will be able to transfer all or part of the difference (see examples above) to your new home.

When you apply for the exemption on your new home, you will have to include a copy of your notice of proposed property taxes on your old home and sign a sworn statement that you are entitled to the assessment reduction.

Adding or Deleting an Owner. If you add or remove an owner from the title of your homestead, it is possible you could lose the Save Our Homes benefit. Changes in ownership will cause the property to be assessed at Market Value as of January 1 of the year following the change of ownership. In our previous example, you will remember that the property had a Market Value of $450,000 but, because of the Save Our Homes Amendment, the taxable value was only $318,270. If you added another name to the deed, the taxable value would jump to the Market Value ($450,000 or more) the next year, creating a disastrous increase in property taxes.

The Florida Attorney General has issued two opinions regarding this matter. The opinions state that adding or deleting a name to or from a deed is a change of ownership. Many residents add the names of one or more of their children to the title of their homestead to avoid probate on their deaths. Most of them don't realize that this is considered a change of ownership and will cause the taxable value of their home to immediately jump up to the market value, resulting in an increase in their property tax. Depending on how long the owner owned the home, the property taxes could double or even triple.

Section 193.155 of the Florida Statutes lists four exceptions to the change of ownership rule:

1. If the change was made to correct an error in the first deed (misspelled name, etc.) or the transfer was between legal and equitable title (transferring the title of the property to the prior owner's revocable trust), the taxable value will not be affected.

2.　　　If the transfer is between husband and wife, including transfer to a surviving spouse or a transfer due to divorce, the taxable value will not be affected.

3.　　　If the transfer is to a surviving spouse as a result of the homestead law after the death of one spouse (see " Legal Restrictions" later in this chapter), the taxable value will not be affected.

4.　　　If the owner dies and the property passes to a permanent resident who is legally or naturally dependent on the owner, the taxable value will not be affected. For example, the owner dies and leaves his property to one or more of his dependent children.

Personal Exemptions. There are other additional exemptions that will reduce the taxable value of the homestead property by $500 per exemption available to qualified Florida residents. Examples of these exemptions are: Widow or widower exemption, Legally Blind persons, and Disabled Veterans. Certain civilians and veterans with total and permanent disabilities may qualify for 100 percent exemption from property taxes. These exemptions are discussed in Chapter 2.

Qualifying for the Homestead Tax Exemption. In order to qualify for the homestead tax exemption you must be an individual, who as of January 1 of the year for which you are filing, must be a permanent resident of Florida, must own and occupy the property as your permanent residence, and must hold title or beneficial interest to the property.

The first of the year date is important. If you move into the house on January 2, meet every other qualification, and spend every moment for the rest of the year in the home, you will not be entitled to the homestead tax exemption. You have to be living there on January 1.

Applying for the Homestead Tax Exemption. If, as of January 1, you meet the qualifications listed above, you may apply for homestead exemption at the property appraiser's office in your county. The property appraiser will provide a form for you to complete. You must sign the application form in person at the appraiser's office. The application must be filed no later than March 1 of the year for which the exemption applies. All persons named on the deed of the property must sign the application, except in the case of husband and wife where only one signature is required. When applying for homestead exemption, each of you must provide proof of ownership of the property and proof of Florida residency.

1. Proof of Ownership. Any of the following items can be presented to show proof of ownership of the property: Deed to the Property (must be recorded in the public records of the county at the time of application), Property Tax Bill, Title Insurance, Contract for Deed, Cooperative Proprietary Lease, Certified Copy of Last Will and Testament (showing that the property was devised to you).

2. Proof of Residency. To show evidence of your Florida residency, you can furnish a valid Florida driver's license or Florida identification card (with the date of issuance on or before January 1) and one or more of the following items: Florida vehicle registration, Declaration of Domicile dated prior to January 1, previous year's filing of your federal income tax return showing a Florida address. If you are a resident alien, a permanent visa card or a temporary visa card with official assurance that permanent residence status is approved must be presented.

The Exemption From Forced Sale and Creditors. Perhaps the most controversial aspect of the

Florida homestead law is its protection from forced sale by creditors.

Quite simply, this means that a Florida resident's homestead is exempt from creditor's claims. Therefore, if you are at fault in an automobile accident, are sued, and a judgment is entered against you, your creditors could not force you to sell your homestead to pay the judgment. Also, the judgment would not become a lien against the homestead property as it would against any other real estate you own.

There are, however, exceptions to the exemption. Liens for ad valorem property taxes and assessments are enforceable against the homestead. Any liens which you voluntarily place against your homestead, such as mortgages, are enforceable. A foreclosure of a mortgage is not a prohibited forced sale under the law. Likewise, liens for improvements made to or repairs made on your homestead are not exempted. Therefore, construction liens (discussed in Chapter 9) are enforceable against your homestead property. Other liens which are not affected by the homestead exemption are code enforcement liens and federal tax liens.

Florida is one of just a few states which allow an unlimited amount for its homestead exemption. It was established in its early years as a state to draw people as residents and to protect families from being rendered homeless in bad financial times. Lately the exemption has been heavily criticized, with the critics claiming that abuses have enabled debtors to declare bankruptcy, and use the homestead exemption to continue to enjoy a life of luxury while their creditors get little or nothing. Some examples that they cite are actor, Burt Reynolds, who declared bankruptcy in 1996, claiming more than ten million dollars in debt. Reynolds was able to keep his $2.5 million estate, named

"Valhalla," while his creditors reportedly received only 20 cents on the dollar. Paul Bilzerian has been able to avoid payment of $200 million owed to his creditors while using the Florida homestead exemption to keep his $5 million dollar home. And of course, most people are aware that O.J. Simpson moved to Florida and purchased a home which was protected from the $33.5 million civil judgment against him over the slayings of his ex-wife and her friend.

Proponents of the homestead exemption point out that despite the outrageousness of some of the abuses, they are a tiny fraction of the bankruptcy filings and the homestead exemption is needed to help people who truly need the protection, such as retirees who become overwhelmed with medical bills or young families who run up too much credit card debt.

Homestead and Bankruptcy. The basic idea most people have of bankruptcy is that a debtor who is unable to pay his obligations files a petition in bankruptcy court and, after the bankruptcy process, his debts are discharged, any judgment liens against him are wiped out and he starts with a clean slate. That is not entirely accurate. While a bankruptcy usually relieves a debtor from personal liability for his debts, it usually does not eliminate all of the rights of secured creditors. Secured creditors are those who have taken a mortgage or other type of lien as security or collateral for the loan or debt. Also, the lien created by a judgment obtained by a creditor against a debtor is not wiped out. As a result, a creditor may still have the right to foreclose on property to satisfy the debt, even though the debtor is no longer personally liable for such debt.

This is where the homestead exemption provides protection. The federal bankruptcy code provides that a debtor may avoid a judicial lien if it impairs an exemption to which the debtor would have been entitled. Therefore, the debtor can avoid in the bankruptcy the lien of a judgment against property that qualifies for the homestead exemption.

However, a person cannot move to Florida and immediately file for bankruptcy to take advantage of the homestead exemption. For the purposes of claiming the homestead exemption in bankruptcy cases, a debtor will be considered domiciled in Florida if he or she has been domiciled in Florida for 180 days before the bankruptcy filing.

As of October, 2005, Federal bankruptcy law places limits on Florida's homestead exemption. The exemption is limited to $125,000 if the debtor had only acquired the property during the 1,215 days prior to filing bankruptcy. Property owned for more than 1,215 days is not affected and retains the entire exemption.

When Does the Exemption Apply? A judgment becomes a lien against the debtor's real estate at the time a certified copy is recorded in the public records of the county where the real estate is located. If the property is not the debtor's homestead at the time the judgment is recorded, then a lien is created at that time. It doesn't matter that the debtor later makes the property his homestead; the validity of the judgment lien is determined at the time of recording. However, if the property is the debtor's homestead at the time of recording, then no lien is created. But if the property later loses its homestead status, the lien would then attach to the property.

It is also possible for the debtor to sell the homestead property and the proceeds of such sale would be exempt from the claims of creditors if the debtor reinvests the proceeds into purchase of another homestead property. In such a case, the proceeds must be kept separate and not commingled with the debtor's other funds.

Restraint on Lifetime Transfer. The third aspect of the Florida homestead law involves the restrictions of the transfer of homestead property. The Florida Constitution and statutes place restrictions on the manner in which homestead can be transferred during the owner's lifetime and devised after his or her death.

During his or her lifetime, if the owner of homestead is married, then his or her spouse must join in any alienation of it. "Alienation" is defined as any transfer, whether by conveyance of an entire (or fee simple) interest, a fractional interest, a mortgage, lease, easement or contract. Therefore, if Mr. Smith is the owner of the Florida homestead property in which he and his wife reside and he wishes to sell the property, then his wife must also sign the deed for the transfer to be valid. This is true, even though Mrs. Smith's name was never on the deed. She would also need to sign any mortgage, lease, easement or sales contract.

This is why, on most deeds transferring Florida property, you will see the marital status of the seller after his or her name. If it states that he or she is single, then homestead status is not important. However, if it states that the seller is married, then the seller's spouse must sign the deed if it is homestead, or the seller must state that the property is not his or her homestead.

Homestead After Death. Florida places restrictions on how a person can leave his property after his death if he is survived by a spouse or minor child. This is important for estate planning purposes because failure to heed these restrictions can result in an ownership nightmare.

This is why I recommend that you not use one of those fill in the blanks wills or trusts that you can purchase from an office supply store or on the internet. You may save some money, but as you're going to see, your family may pay dearly for years to come.

What happens to your homestead after your death centers on three different issues: 1) is the property your homestead? 2) how does the homestead pass to your next generation? and 3) is the homestead free from the claims of your creditors?

Is It Homestead Property? The same definition we used earlier to determine if property is homestead property is also the definition used to determine whether the property is homestead at the time of death. That definition, as discussed earlier in this chapter, is real property, of no more than 160 contiguous acres outside a municipality, or no more than one half an acre of contiguous land in a municipality, owned by a natural person, and the house and other improvements on it.

If the property meets these qualifications the homestead law applies. If not, then the property is treated the same as any other asset in your estate. In probate proceedings your personal representative (or executor) can ask the court to determine if the property is homestead.

Legal Restrictions. If you are married, the Florida Constitution does not allow you to leave your homestead to anyone other than your surviving spouse. If you have a minor child, things get really complicated. Therefore, how you can dispose of your homestead in your will is dependent on whether or not you are married or have a minor child at the time of death. If you are not survived by a spouse or minor child, you may devise the property in any manner you wish. The term devise means transfer according to the terms of a will or trust. If you have a spouse but no minor child, you may devise the homestead only to your spouse. In addition, the devise to your spouse must be of your entire interest in the homestead property. If you have a minor child, you cannot devise the homestead property at all.

The next obvious question is: What happens if the owner tries to devise the homestead other than allowed?

If you are survived by a spouse and have a provision in your will or trust which tries to leave the homestead to anyone other than your surviving spouse, the provisions of the will are disregarded by law, your spouse takes a life estate (she owns the property for a term ending at the time of her death) in the homestead, with a vested remainder to your lineal descendants (at the death of your spouse, title to the homestead immediately passes to your children who were alive at the date of your death). Under these circumstances your surviving spouse only has ownership for the remainder of her life. As a result she can only transfer the same interest to a third party. For example, if your surviving spouse sells her interest in the homestead to her friend and dies a week later, the friend's interest would terminate at your spouse's death and title would pass to your lineal descendants. This creates the unintended situation where the surviving spouse must obtain the consent of your lineal descendants if she wishes to sell or mortgage the homestead. If you would have left his entire interest in the homestead to your surviving spouse, then the surviving spouse would not have a life estate but full fee simple title with authority to sell and mortgage as she pleased.

If husband and wife own the homestead property together as tenants by the entireties, the restrictions do not apply, and upon the death of one, the surviving spouse has full interest in the property. This is the case even when there is a minor child. For this reason, married couples with a minor child should almost always own their homestead as husband and wife, as tenants by the entireties.

Claims of Creditors. Upon your death, the assets of your probate estate are used to pay any debts that you owed at the time of death, as well as expenses of administration. The probate estate generally consists of assets in your sole name, which contain no provision for automatic succession of ownership at death (such as beneficiary designations). This includes personal property owned by you wherever located and real estate located in Florida, except homestead.

The Florida Constitution provides that your spouse or heirs benefit from the homestead exemption. In other words, your exemption from forced sale by creditors passes to your surviving spouse or heirs. The term "heirs" in this context means those persons who would take your property if you died intestate (without a will). These are usually your lineal descendants such as children and grandchildren. See Chapter 4 for a discussion of intestate succession.

Therefore, if you devise your homestead to your spouse or to your heirs that would receive it had there been no will, then your creditors cannot reach the homestead and the property passes "free of the claims of creditors."

If the homestead is devised to persons other than your surviving spouse or heirs (such as a good friend), it is subject to the claims of creditors and is treated as a part of the probate estate.

If you direct in your will that the homestead be sold and the proceeds distributed, then the proceeds are not exempt from the claims of your creditors, even if such proceeds would be distributed to your heirs.

Marital Agreements. Lucy is a widow whose previous husband left her their homestead when he died with the expectation that she leave it to their children upon her death. A few months ago, Lucy met Ricky and the two of them are engaged to be married. Both Lucy and Ricky are financially self-sufficient and each wishes to leave his or her inheritance to their respective children. After the wedding they plan to live in Lucy's home. Lucy is concerned because she read that Florida law requires her to devise her homestead to her husband. What can Lucy and Ricky do to insure that their estates go to their children, especially that Lucy's homestead goes to hers? Under Florida law, they can waive their homestead rights by a written pre-nuptial (pre-marital) agreement. Under this agreement, Ricky gives up his rights to the homestead property and, assuming Lucy has no minor child, allows Lucy to devise the homestead in any manner she chooses. An agreement may be entered into after the marriage, but full and fair disclosure of each person's assets must be included in such case and many title companies require that a determination from a court that the post-nuptial agreement is valid be obtained.

It is important to realize that a valid pre-marital agreement will not allow the owner of the homestead to sell it during his or her lifetime without the joinder of the spouse.

QUICK REVIEW OF HOMESTEAD

1.   Homestead is real property no larger than 160 acres outside of a municipality and one-half an acre inside a municipality owned by a natural person.

2.   The owner must reside on the homestead property.

3.   The owner's spouse must join in on any contract, deed or mortgage transferring any interest in the homestead.

4.   Homestead is exempt from forced sale by creditors, with certain limited exceptions.

5.   Homestead may not be devised if the owner has a minor child.

6.   If the owner is married and does not have a minor child, homestead may only be devised to the spouse, unless the spouse has waived all rights in the homestead by a valid marital agreement.

7.   If the homestead is devised to the decedent's heirs, it will pass to them free of the claims of creditors.

CHAPTER 4

Probate in Florida

As a new Florida resident, you should know that your property may be treated differently after your death than it would have in your previous state. Florida's probate process is a very thorough system designed to pass a person's possessions to his or her heirs. While it is thorough, it is often not very efficient. Probate has been known to test the fortitude of even the most patient beneficiaries. But once you understand the procedure and the reasons for probate, it becomes a tolerable process.

Simply defined, probate is the procedure necessary to establish the validity of a will. The process of collecting a decedent's assets, paying his bills and taxes, and distributing what is left to his heirs or beneficiaries is actually called "administration" of the estate although it has become common to refer to this entire process as probate.

There are two types of probate administration under Florida law: formal administration and summary administration. Formal administration is what most people tend to consider a "probate." Summary administration is an abbreviated proceeding for smaller estates. Summary administration is available if the gross value of the probate estate is not greater than $75,000 or if the decedent has been dead for at least two years.

Estates can be either testate, where the decedent has left a valid will, or intestate, where there is no will. In an administration of an intestate estate the laws of the state of Florida will determine how the assets are distributed. In a testate estate, the will acts as a set of instructions to the court, naming a personal representative and directing the disposition of the assets.

Estates subject to probate administration consist of assets owned solely by the decedent with no provision for automatic succession of ownership at death. Examples of automatic succession include the following:

- Beneficiary designations on life insurance policies and annuity contracts,
- "Transfer on death" or "payable on death" provisions on financial and brokerage accounts,
- Bank accounts held "in trust for" a beneficiary and property owned as joint tenants with a right of survivorship.

These assets would not be included in a probate estate and generally would go automatically to the named beneficiary or surviving joint tenant.

Formal Administration. Any estate, regardless of size, can utilize the Formal Administration procedure in Florida. If the value of the probatable assets of the estate exceeds $75,000 and the decedent has been dead for less than two years, formal administration is required. In determining the estate's value, non-probatable assets are not included. Non-probatable assets are those with automatic succession of ownership at death (see examples above), property owned in a trust, exempt property (household furnishings with a net value up to $10,000, automobiles, pre-paid college funds and $1,000 worth of personal property) and homestead property. Also, the word "value" refers to the gross as opposed to net value of the estate. This means that a $200,000 house with a mortgage of $100,000 has a value of $200,000 for the purposes of the probate law.

Production of Will. Florida law requires that the person who is in custody of the Will must deposit it with the Clerk of Court in the county where the decedent resided within 10 days after receiving information that the decedent is dead.

Opening Formal Administration. Formal administration is started by filing a Petition for Administration. The Petition for Administration provides the Courts with basic information it needs to open the estate. It identifies the decedent, states the approximate nature and value of the estate assets, names the beneficiaries, requests appointment of a Personal Representative, and, in a testate estate, identifies the Will and requests that it be admitted to probate. All interested persons (as defined by Florida law) must then be served with formal notice of the petition. If the court finds the petition to be in order and there are no objections to the petition, then the Will is admitted to probate and the Personal Representative is appointed and issued Letters of Administration. The Letters of Administration give the Personal Representative authority granted by the court to act on behalf of the estate.

Appointment of the Personal Representative. In a testate estate (one with a will), the court will give preference to the person nominated in the decedent's Will as the Personal Representative, if such person is qualified to act. Any person who is at least 18 years of age and who is a resident of Florida at the time of the decedent's death may qualify as the Personal Representative. A person who is not a resident of Florida cannot qualify unless he or she is

1) the decedent's children, grandchildren or other lineal descendant, parent, grandparent or other lineal ascendant,

2) the decedent's legally adopted child or adoptive parent,

3) the decedent's spouse, brother, sister, uncle, aunt, nephew or niece, 4) a lineal descendant or ascendant of any person described in 3), or

5) the spouse of anyone otherwise listed above.

All trust companies incorporated under Florida law can also qualify.

If the person nominated in the Will cannot qualify and an alternate personal representative who can qualify is named in the Will, then the alternate may be appointed.

If there is no Will (the estate is intestate), then preference in appointment of the Personal Representative is governed by the Florida Probate Code. The order of preference set forth in the statute is as follows:

1) the surviving spouse,

2) the person selected by a majority in interest of the heirs, or

3) the heir closest in relation to the decedent.

The court may require that a fiduciary bond be posted in order for the Personal Representative to be appointed. The bond is to protect the beneficiaries and creditors of the estate and is conditioned on the performance by the Personal Representative of all his or her duties under law. The court may require that a bond be posted even if the Will specifically waives bond. This is especially true in the instances where the Personal Representative is not a resident of Florida.

Once appointed by the court, the Personal Representative then publishes a Notice of Administration and a Notice to Creditors once a week for 2 consecutive weeks in a newspaper of general circulation in the county where the estate is administered. The Notice to Creditors is intended to notify creditors of the decedent of the administration of the estate so that they may file claims to have any outstanding debts of the decedent paid. The Personal Representative is also required to serve a copy of the notice on those creditors of which he is aware. As a general rule, the creditors must file a claim with the court within 3 months of the date of the first publication or they will lose all rights to collect their debt.

Estate Assets and Inventory. The Personal Representative is responsible for identifying and collecting the estate assets. The probate estate assets consist of personal property owned by the decedent wherever located, and real estate owned by the decedent in Florida, except homestead. The Personal Representative is responsible for obtaining the value of the property and preparing and filing an inventory of the property with the court.

The inventory consists of a complete listing of the probate estate assets and the value of each asset. The value shall be the estimated fair market value of the assets on the decedent's date of death. Only gross values are reported and any mortgages or other encumbrances are disregarded. The inventory is kept confidential by the court. After filing with the court, the personal representative must send a copy of the inventory to the Florida Department of Revenue, the surviving spouse and each heir or beneficiary. The law requires that the personal representative file the inventory within 60 days after the Letters of Administration have been issued.

Creditor's Claims. Almost every estate has creditors. For example, credit card companies, doctors and hospitals are creditors. Also, the funeral home is a creditor to the extent of services performed. There may be additional estate creditors. However, except for the funeral claim, claims are limited to amounts which were owed (even though not yet billed) by the decedent as of the moment of death. It is easy to understand this by assuming what the decedent would have paid if death had not intervened. Debts which are incurred after death in connection with the estate administration are not included in this category and are handled in another manner.

As noted above, the Personal Representative is required to publish a Notice to Creditors and mail a copy of such notice to each creditor that can reasonably be identified. The Notice to Creditors advises all persons having claims or demands against the estate to file their claims with the court within three months after the time of the first publication of the notice. This time until the deadline is known as the "claims period."

If the creditor does not file a Statement of Claim with the court within the claims period, they will lose all rights to enforce and collect the claim or debt.

At the end of the claims period, the Personal Representative should investigate all claims against the estate and object to those he or she determines to be invalid. Objections to claims must be filed with the court before the later of four months after the first publication of the Notice to Creditors or thirty days after the timely filing of the claim, and must be mailed to the person making the claim. If the Personal Representative does not file a timely objection, the claim must be paid.

Closing the Estate. After the claims period has expired and all claims have either been paid or barred, and after all taxes, if any, due from the estate have been paid, the Personal Representative is ready to begin the procedure to close the estate.

The first step in closing the estate is the filing of a final accounting. The final accounting is a report that includes all cash and property transactions since the opening of the probate administration. In estates where there are a small number of beneficiaries or all beneficiaries are close family members, the beneficiaries may wish to waive the filing of the final accounting. If not waived, the final accounting must be filed with the court and served on all interested persons within 12 months after the Letters of Administration have been issued. If an estate is large enough that a federal estate tax return is required to be filed, the time for filing may be extended to 12 months after the date the tax return is due.

At this time, the Personal Representative must also file a Petition for Discharge and serve it on all interested parties. The petition must state that the estate has been fully administered and that all taxes and expenses of administration have been paid or provision has been made to pay them. It must show the amount of compensation paid or to be paid to the Personal Representative and the attorney for the Personal Representative and show how the assets of the estate are to be distributed.

If no objections to the petition are filed, the Personal Representative may distribute the estate property. When the court is satisfied that the estate has been fully administered and properly distributed, it will enter an order discharging the Personal Representative and releasing the surety on any bond. At this time, the Personal Representative is released from his or her duties and liabilities.

Compensation of the Personal Representative and Attorney. The Personal Representative, attorney for the estate and other professionals involved in the administration of the estate are entitled by law to be paid for their services. Florida law states that the personal representative may receive a commission payable from the estate assets based upon the value of the estate. Section 733.617 of the Florida Probate Code provides a schedule of fees which is "presumed to be reasonable compensation for the personal representative.

Estate Value	Percentage Fee
Up to $1 million	3%
$1 million to 5 million	2 1/2%
$5 million to 10 million	2%
portion of estate exceeding	
$10 million	1 1/2%

The Probate Code also addresses reasonable amounts for fees for the attorney for the personal representative.

Elective Share. In Florida, a person cannot cut his or her spouse out of an inheritance. Florida law has provisions that gave a surviving spouse a portion of the deceased spouse's estate so that the survivor is not disinherited and left destitute. This is called the "Elective Share Law."

When the Elective Share Law was enacted in 1975, it provided that a surviving spouse was entitled to a minimum of a 30% share of the deceased spouse's probate estate. Under the law, the surviving spouse had the option of accepting what was provided under the decedent's will, or electing to take a 30% share of the decedent's net probate assets. The Elective Share did not apply to assets passing outside of probate. Since a large number of people set up trusts, transfer on death arrangements, and other vehicles to avoid probate, some estates had no probate assets. As a result, many surviving spouses were either inadvertently or intentionally disinherited.

In response to this problem, the Florida legislature passed a new bill which was signed into law on June 11, 1999, by Governor Jeb Bush, that completely revamped the Elective Share law. The new law closes the loophole by including in the Elective Share assets that do not pass through probate as well as the decedent's probate estate. The new, larger estate subject to the elective share is referred to as the "augmented estate" or "Elective Estate." Property included in the Elective Estate includes the value of:

- the decedent's probate estate
- bank accounts and investment accounts titled jointly with a right of survivorship, as well as transfer on death accounts and other similar arrangements.
- The decedent's interest in property held as joint tenants or tenants by the entireties.
- Assets held in revocable trusts established by the decedent
- Transfers of property by the decedent in which the decedent retained a right to income or principal.
- Cash surrender value of life insurance policies on the decedent's life (not the value of the death benefits).

- Pensions and Individual Retirement Accounts.
- Gifts and certain transfers of property out of the decedent's estate within one year prior to death.
- Transfers of property made to satisfy the Elective Share.

The surviving spouse is entitled to elect to take an "elective share" which is 30% of the value of the Elective Estate. Once this amount is calculated, the statute sets forth the procedure to satisfy the Elective Share or the law will direct how it is paid. Either way the surviving spouse will receive the 30% share.

In second marriages or other situations where an Elective Share election is not desirable, it is possible for the spouses to waive their right to make an Elective Share election by a pre or post-marital agreement.

Summary Administration. As we have discussed, formal administration is an expensive and time consuming procedure that leaves many beneficiaries and personal representatives frustrated. What if an estate was forced to go through probate even if the only asset was a single share of stock or a small bank account? In such a case, the fees and costs of probate might exceed the value of the estate.

For these situations, Florida has a couple of procedures intended to simplify and drastically reduce the time and expense of probate. In both cases there is no appointment of a personal representative and the estate is usually distributed in a matter of weeks instead of a minimum of five months.

Summary Administration is available for estates (subject to probate) whose gross value does not exceed $75,000 or when the decedent has been dead for longer than two years. In determining whether the decedent's estate qualifies for Summary Administration, the value of the estate does not include non-probatable assets (this term is defined earlier in this chapter). It also does not include homestead or exempt property such as household furnishings, automobiles, college savings plans and personal property valued up to $1,000.

Summary Administration is also available when the decedent has been dead for more than two years, even if the value of the estate exceeds $75,000. This is because there is a two-year statute of limitations for creditors to file claims against the decedent's estate after his or her death. After the two years have expired, there is no need to go through the claims procedure of formal administration.

To probate an estate under Summary Administration, an interested person, usually a beneficiary of the estate, files a Petition for Summary Administration with the probate court. The petition must be signed by the surviving spouse and any beneficiaries. It contains facts showing that Summary Administration is proper in this case, information about the decedent, information about the surviving spouse and beneficiaries, a description of the assets, and a proposed schedule of distribution.

In most cases the court does not require a hearing. If the petition is proper and the court determines that Summary Administration is warranted, the judge will sign an Order of Summary Administration which names the beneficiaries and how they are to receive their share of the estate.

When an Order of Summary Administration is issued, the beneficiaries become personally liable (up to the value of the assets they received) for all lawful claims against the estate. To protect the beneficiaries, one may publish in a local newspaper, a notice to creditors. The creditors then have three months to file a claim against the estate or their right to do so is barred forever.

In cases where the value of probatable assets is less than the sum of the amount of the decedent's funeral expenses and reasonable and necessary medical and hospital expenses of the last 60 days of the decedent's last illness, a procedure known as Disposition Without Administration may be obtained. This procedure does not require the assistance of an attorney and is made by an interested party filling out and signing a form obtained from the clerk of court. The form requests distribution of the assets according to a will, if testate, or by law if intestate.

Ancillary Administration. Any real estate located in the state of Florida is under the jurisdiction of the state of Florida regardless of where the owner lived. So, if a resident of a state other than Florida dies and leaves real estate located in Florida, the probate in his state of residence will not transfer the title of the Florida property to his heirs or devisees. There will need to be a proceeding in Florida, known as Ancillary Administration, to probate the Florida property.

Let's say Joe, a resident of Illinois, owns a winter home in Florida. Joe dies and his estate is probated in Illinois. Since Illinois is Joe's state of residence, the probate proceedings in Illinois are referred to as the "Domiciliary Administration." Joe's best friend, Tom, also a resident of Illinois, acts as Joe's Personal Representative or executor in the Domiciliary Administration. He is called the "Domiciliary Personal Representative." Tom's appointment by the Illinois court as Personal Representative does not give him any authority to act in Florida. A Personal Representative will have to be appointed by the Florida courts to deal with the

Florida real estate. This person is referred to as the "Ancillary Personal Representative."

Usually the Domiciliary Personal Representative will apply to the Florida court to have Ancillary Letters of Administration issued to him. However, in this case Tom does not qualify to act a Personal Representative in Florida since he is neither a resident of Florida nor related to Joe. If Joe's Will nominates an alternate Personal Representative who qualifies, that person will be appointed by the court; otherwise, those entitled to a majority interest in the Florida property may select a Personal Representative.

The Domiciliary Personal Representative, a beneficiary or any other interested party may file a Petition for Ancillary Administration. It contains a copy, authenticated by the domiciliary court, of the Will and other documents of the domiciliary probate proceeding. If the Florida court determines that the Will complies with Florida law, it will admit the Will to probate and issue Ancillary Letters of Administration to the Ancillary Personal Representative. The Ancillary Administration then proceeds the same as a regular Florida formal administration, with notification of creditors, payment of claims, inventory, accounting and distribution of the property. The court may order the Florida property held by the Ancillary Personal Representative to be transferred to the Domiciliary Personal Representative or distributed directly to the beneficiaries.

If You Are Acting as Personal Representative of a Florida Estate. If you are chosen to act as a Personal Representative in Florida, it is a job you should not take lightly. Administering an estate takes more work and time than most people realize. The job description of Personal

Representative includes accountant, investor, manager and, in many cases, emotional counsellor and referee.

You need to choose a Florida attorney experienced in probate matters who you can work with. A good attorney will be able to explain the process to you and make the job much easier.

For the period of administration of the estate you are entitled to possession and control of all of the assets of the estate. Your duty is first and foremost to protect and preserve the assets and also to see that the assets are invested in a prudent and cautious manner.

The persons to whom you owe these duties are, first, any creditors of the estate, and second, the beneficiaries of the estate. If your duties are not properly or competently performed, you may have to answer to any of these persons who have been harmed as a result.

Throughout the estate proceeding, management of the assets is an important concern of the Personal Representative. Management of the assets includes investment of the assets, whether in bank accounts, government bonds, or other prudent forms of investment, to the extent that the estate has excess cash. A further and important consideration is liquidity management. The Personal Representative is required to sell assets or borrow money on behalf of the estate to meet the cash requirements as they arise, if cash available to the estate is not otherwise sufficient. Cash requirements for the estate include the payment of creditors, the payment of expenses of administration, and the payment of taxes.

As Personal Representative of the estate, in accepting that office and that trust, you have also agreed to be personally responsible financially for certain matters. Initially, of course, you have personal responsibility for proper administration, investment, and subsequent distribution of the assets of the estate. As I pointed out earlier, should you fail in this duty you may be sued by any person who has been injured by your failure. More important, however, is certain hidden liability which you have assumed, and of which you should be aware, for the payment of various taxes that were owed by the decedent, or that may subsequently be owed by the estate. Upon the failure to pay these required taxes, the law permits the Internal Revenue Service, and in some situations, the State of Florida, to collect the taxes from your own assets. This would include the right to freeze your personal bank account or place liens on real estate or other property which may belong to you personally. This, of course, occurs only if you failed to pay taxes from the estate that are required to be paid by you in your capacity as personal representative. It is because of this exposure to items that might otherwise be unknown to you that you should work closely with your attorney, and you should permit your attorney to advise you at each level on your duties and responsibilities. Also, if you have any questions or are unsure about any action you may take, you should not proceed without your attorney's advice.

CHAPTER 5

Estate Planning in Florida

After moving to Florida, it is always a good idea to have your Will and other estate planning documents reviewed by a Florida attorney. As I mentioned previously, your Will should state that you are a Florida resident and your estate plan should comply with Florida law. If you don't already have an estate plan, now is the time to consider one. You saw in the last chapter how expensive and time consuming probate in Florida can be.

Estate planning is simply the process of structuring your estate in a way to direct how your assets get to the persons you want to receive them in the most efficient manner. It can be as elaborate as setting up a myriad of trusts and foundations or as uncomplicated as writing a simple Will or even doing nothing at all. In Florida, there is a bumper sticker that is popular with many retirees. It says: "I'm Spending My Children's Inheritance." Unfortunately, in many cases, that is the full extent of their estate planning. It has been estimated that a vast majority of our country's population has done no estate planning; not even a simple Will. In those cases, their estate planning will be done by the laws of the state in which they reside. In some cases things will turn out the way that they would have wanted. However, in many cases it will not.

Is My Massachusetts Will Valid in Florida? A problem that can arise is when persons have their Wills and other estate planning documents prepared "up north" and move to Florida. In many cases they rely on the documents as they were drawn up originally without having a Florida attorney review them. Every state has its own distinct and different laws regarding probate and other estate planning matters. Once you become a resident of Florida, your Will must comply with Florida law. A document drawn in another state may not be valid in Florida or, if it is valid, may not be interpreted the same way as originally intended. Florida law requires Wills to be in writing and to be executed by the testator (person making the Will) in the presence of two witnesses who then must sign the Will in the presence of the testator and of each other.

Florida also provides that a Will may be self-proved. This happens when the testator (testatrix, if female) and the witnesses acknowledge the Will and execute a self-proving affidavit in the presence of a notary. Any Will that is self-proved may be admitted to probate without testimony of the attending witnesses. Many states do not customarily self-prove wills. In these cases the witnesses must be found and they must sign an oath before a judge, clerk or deputy clerk, or court-appointed commissioner, that the Will being offered for probate is the same Will he witnessed the decedent sign. Imagine trying to track down the person who witnessed your Will 40 years ago in Illinois.

For these reasons, and because you want your Will to state that you are a resident of Florida, you should have your out-of-state Will reviewed by a Florida attorney, and in most cases, you should have a new Florida Will prepared.

What exactly is a Will, and Doesn't It Avoid Probate? A Will is a document that gives instructions to the Personal Representative and the probate court as to how your assets will pass to your heirs and beneficiaries after your death. Any assets that pass to your heirs through a Will are guaranteed to go through probate. Your Will should have four main parts. The first is the nomination of a "Personal Representative" (sometimes called an executor in other states) who will manage and administer your estate after your death. You may also appoint someone to serve as guardian for your minor children. The second is the statement directing how your assets will be distributed to your beneficiaries. The third part of the Will specifies any special powers or authority that the Personal Representative will have to administer the estate. These powers include the power to sell real estate without court approval. Finally, there is the execution portion of the Will. This is where the testator (man who makes the will) or the testatrix (woman who makes the will) signs the document as his or her Last Will and Testament and where the attesting witnesses also sign the Will. It may also contain a self-proving affidavit as described earlier.

Advantages of a Will. A Will provides a plan for distributing your assets at the time of your death and allows you to decide who will be the Personal Representative of your estate. The Will is a pro-active method of planning your estate and gives you a large degree of control as to what happens to your assets after you are gone.

Disadvantages of a Will. A Will does not avoid probate. Any assets passing through the Will are subject to the costs, delays and lack of privacy of the probate process.

Generally, probate administration costs between 4% and 8% of the total gross value of the portion of your estate passing through probate. These costs include Personal Representative fees, attorney's fees, court costs and publication fees. Probate administration also takes a minimum of five months to complete and it is not unusual for a typical estate to drag on for a year or longer. Finally, probate proceedings are a matter of public record. Anyone can find out who your estate is distributed to and, even though the inventory of your estate is not open to the public, there are methods for finding out what assets are in your estate and the value.

Also, a Will only becomes valid at your death. It does not address incapacity during your lifetime. An estate plan that only consists of a Will does not prevent the necessity of a guardianship if you are unable to manage your affairs during your lifetime.

Avoiding Probate. If you wish to avoid probate, your estate planning must consist of something more than a Will. The following is a list of tools you can use to leave certain assets to your heirs without probate.

Transfer on Death. Transfer on Death (also commonly referred to as "TOD") is a form of securities registration that allows you to name one or more beneficiaries to whom your securities account would pass at your death. The brokerage firm or other entity that accepts the Transfer on Death registration agrees to deliver the securities according to your direction. Any assets passing to a beneficiary as a result of a TOD registration are outside of the probate estate and thus avoid probate.

Advantages of Transfer on Death. TOD registration allows you to maintain complete control of assets during your life and provide for the distribution, outside of probate, to the persons of your choice after your death. The beneficiaries have no ownership interest in the securities during your lifetime. In fact, you can change the TOD designation at any time prior to your death.

Disadvantages of Transfer on Death. TOD only covers assets registered or held in the TOD account. Assets owned outside of TOD accounts must be dealt with in another manner. TOD only takes affect at your death. As with a Will, TOD will not help you if you become incapacitated. Also, the entire account is distributed outright upon your death. If you have minor children or beneficiaries who, for one reason or another, cannot manage money, and you want to have the money managed for their benefit, you should not use a TOD.

"In Trust For" "In Trust For" designations at banks and other financial institutions are similar to TOD accounts in that you can name a person or persons to receive the funds in your account after your death and avoid probate. This designation is generally used for checking account, savings accounts and certificates of deposit. The "In Trust For" designation has the same advantages and disadvantages as Transfer on Death.

Joint Ownership. It is very common in Florida for a surviving spouse to add the name of a child to a deed or to an account or other asset in order to avoid probate. If the ownership is created properly and provides that the property is owned as "joint tenants with right of survivorship," then the asset will pass to the survivor upon the first to die. Although this method avoids probate, it may cause more problems than it solves.

Gift Tax. The addition of your child's name on the asset is a transfer of at least half of the property by gift. It may be subject to gift tax if it is large enough. Also the gift does not provide a "stepped-up basis" to your child for tax purposes. If your child would have received the ownership of the asset as a result of your death, then his or her "basis" in the property would be the value of the property at your death. The basis is "stepped-up" from your basis in the property (the value at the time you acquired it plus any capital improvements you made to the asset). However, because your child received the property as a result of a gift, he or she will also acquire your basis in the property. If the property has increased in value during your ownership, this will mean that your child will realize a greater capital gain as a result of the gift and increased capital gains taxes.

As an example, Mr. Smith purchased a rental property in 1980 for $60,000. In 2003, Mr. Smith wants to add his daughter to the title to avoid probate. The day after adding his daughter, Mr. Smith dies. The property is worth $200,000. Mr. Smith's daughter receives the property without probate and immediately sells it for $200,000. Since she received the property as a gift, her basis is the same as her father's, $60,000. Therefore her capital gain is $140,000 which, at a 15% capital gains tax rate, incurs $21,000 in taxes. If Mr. Smith would have transferred the property to a revocable Trust and named his daughter as the beneficiary of the rental property, she would have received the property without probate, her basis would have been the value at the time of her father's death, $200,000. She would have no capital gain and no taxes as a result of the sale.

Liability. By putting your daughter's name on the asset, you have added her liabilities to the property. If your daughter is in an automobile accident, is sued as a result and has a judgment entered against her, that judgment can become a lien against your property. Her creditors may be able to attach the jointly held property as a means of satisfying her debt. This also applies to bank and investment accounts.

Loss of Control. Also, if your daughter is joint tenant on a parcel of real estate, you cannot sell the property or even put a mortgage on it without her approval and joinder on the deed or mortgage. Even worse, if the jointly held asset is a bank account or investment account, she may be able to sell, liquidate or transfer the asset without your approval or even without your knowledge. You're saying, "I trust my daughter. I know she would completely cooperate with my wishes and wouldn't do anything that was not in my best interest." While this may be true, consider what would happen if your daughter gets a divorce or becomes incapacitated. Would her ex-husband claim any interest in your property? Who would be appointed as her guardian or have authority to act in her behalf if she was unable?

Loss of Homestead. If the property you are adding your daughter's name to is homestead, the change in title may cause you to lose at least a part of your homestead exemption, and would cause your property to be revalued for property tax purposes and cause you to lose the advantage of the "Save Our Homes" Amendment. Depending on how long you have owned your home, it could cause your property taxes to double and possibly even triple.

These disadvantages only apply if you are adding someone other than your spouse to your title. Property owned by husband and wife (or as tenants by the entireties) would be treated completely different than the examples described above. Property owned as tenants by the entirety cannot be attached by creditors of only one spouse. The creditor must have a claim or judgment against both spouses. Adding a spouse to homestead property will not cause a loss in the homestead exemption nor will it affect the value under the "Save Our Homes" Amendment.

No Survivor. Finally, if both joint tenants die in a common accident, there is no survivor to maintain title to the property. The property will, in that case, go through probate.

Annuities, IRAs and Life Insurance. Annuities, Individual Retirement Accounts, life insurance policies, pension plans and other retirement plans provide that the owner may name beneficiaries who would receive the proceeds of the asset upon the death of the owner. The transfers to the beneficiaries would be paid by contract and avoid probate. Most of these assets will also allow you to name a contingent beneficiary if the primary beneficiary named does not survive you. If none of the beneficiaries that you name survive you, then the proceeds will be paid to your probate estate.

The Revocable Trust. The mechanism for avoiding probate that offers the most flexibility is the revocable Trust. A Trust is a legal arrangement in which one party holds the property of another party for the benefit of a third party. While this definition may not make a whole lot of sense to you now, we will revisit it when we discuss how the Trust works. Quite simply, when you set up a Trust for estate planning purposes, you create an entity that will own your property. Because your property is now owned by this entity and not you, when you die or become incapacitated, there is no estate to probate. All of the property remains in the Trust and will be managed or distributed according to the terms of the Trust.

Even though you no longer own the property individually, you will have complete control over the property in the Trust. In fact, overall you will have a greater control because the property will not come under the control of a court appointed personal representative or guardian at the time of your death or incapacity.

Probably the easiest way to describe how a Trust works is to talk about the different persons involved in the Trust. Let's look back to our initial definition of a Trust. "A legal arrangement in which one party holds the property of another party for the benefit of a third party." If we insert the terms of each of the parties it would look like this: "A legal arrangement in which *a Trustee* holds the property of *a Grantor* for the benefit of *a Beneficiary.*"

The first person involved in the Trust that we will discuss is the Grantor. The Grantor is the creator of the Trust. You are the Grantor of your Trust. As the Grantor, you have the right to set up the Trust as you wish. You will determine who will manage the Trust, how the Trust property will be administered and to whom the property will ultimately be distributed. As Grantor, you also have the right to make changes or amendments to the Trust. If circumstances change in the future or if you just change your mind about some provision of the Trust, you can amend it. You can even go as far as revoking the Trust in its entirety. The Grantor is the only person who can amend the Trust. Upon your death, no one else can make changes to the Trust and your wishes must be carried out.

The second person involved in the Trust is the Trustee. The Trustee is the person who manages or administers the Trust. In most cases you will also be the Trustee of the Trust. Therefore as Grantor, you have complete control over the terms and provisions of the Trust, and as the Trustee you control the management of the property in the Trust. As a result you will probably not notice any difference in dealing with your assets within the Trust than before you set up the

Trust. You will have complete control of your assets and will not be restricted in what you can do with them.

If you should become incapacitated or upon your death, a Successor Trustee, who you have selected, will step up and manage the Trust assets in your place. You can appoint almost anyone you wish to serve as your Successor Trustee. It can be a spouse, relative, friend or trust company. You would appoint the Successor Trustee at the time you create and execute the Trust. The Successor Trustee would, at the time of your incapacity, resignation or death, have the authority to manage the Trust assets pursuant to the terms of the Trust.

If your Successor Trustee steps up as a result of your incapacity, he would make sure that your investments are properly managed, that your other assets are cared for, that your bills are paid and that you are cared for in the manner that is necessary and customary to meet your needs. The Successor Trustee cannot take any of your property or income for his own benefit unless you authorize it or it is specifically authorized in the Trust.

If the Successor Trustee takes over as a result of your death, he would manage and distribute the property in the Trust according to the instructions set forth in the Trust. The Trustee is the holder of legal title to the assets that you put into the Trust. If Trust property is to be sold, purchased, encumbered or given away, the Trustee is the one who executes these transactions.

The third person involved in the Trust is the Beneficiary. As the name indicates, the Beneficiary is the person (or persons) who receives the benefits of the Trust. During your lifetime, you will be the Beneficiary of your Trust. All income that is earned by the assets of the Trust (such as dividends from stocks, interest from bonds and certificates of deposit and rent from real estate) is available to you to do as you please. You may spend this income, invest it or even give it away. Again the Trust does not create any restrictions. You will also pay tax on the income just as you did prior to creating the Trust. A revocable Trust will have no effect on your income taxes. Since the taxpayer identification number of the Trust is your social security number and all income is reported under it, the IRS won't even know that you have a Trust. And, believe it or not, they won't even care.

At the time of your death, the beneficiaries then become those persons to whom you have designated your estate to be distributed. Your Trust provisions can specify that your beneficiaries receive their share outright or it can be held in trust for them. The method of distribution you decide can be extremely flexible. If a beneficiary's share is held in trust, the Trustee will manage and invest the assets and distribute them according to the terms of the Trust. You may direct that only income from the share be paid to the beneficiary, or that principal installments be paid on certain dates, or that the beneficiary receive the share upon reaching a certain age or upon a certain event such as marriage, graduation from college or entering into a business. You can make the distribution provisions very strict or you may give the Trustee a large amount of discretion.

The Trust can also contain provisions regarding distribution to a contingent beneficiary in cases where the primary beneficiary predeceases the Grantor. For example, you may want to leave a portion of your estate to your brother, but you can provide that, if your brother does not survive you, his share will be distributed among his children. You can also specify that, if his children are minors or incapacitated, the Trustee will hold their shares until they reach a certain age at which time it will be distributed to them. If your brother survives you, then he will receive his entire share.

Estate Tax Savings. A revocable Trust can also be used to eliminate or minimize the amount of estate tax that will be due upon your death. The Internal Revenue Code states that, in 2008, any individual may pass $2,000,000 to his heirs without any estate tax due. This credit against estate tax is called the unified credit. In addition, if you are married when you die, you can take advantage of the unlimited marital deduction. This means that you can leave as much of your estate to your spouse, outright or in trust, and it will not be subject to federal estate tax. If you leave it to your spouse in trust, the only requirement is that you must give your spouse the right to all of the income generated by the property.

By combining the unified credit with the unlimited marital deduction, it is possible for a married couple to leave $4 million to their heirs without estate taxes.

Let's take the case of Fred and Wilma. Fred and Wilma are both in their second marriage. Fred came into the marriage with $500,000 in assets and Wilma brought $2.5 million. The two have agreed that after they have both passed away, they want Fred's children to receive $500,000 and Wilma's children to get $2.5 million. Wilma wants to provide for Fred if she should die first, but still wants her children to receive the $2.5 million after his death. Also, neither wants to pay any federal estate tax.

To accomplish this, Fred and Wilma had their estate planning attorney create a revocable Trust for each of them. The Trust provided that upon the death of one, if the spouse survived, an amount of the deceased spouse's estate equal to the unified credit would be set aside in a trust called the "credit shelter" trust. The remaining amount, if any, would be held in a second trust called the "marital deduction" trust. The Trust document provided that all income from both trusts would be paid to the surviving spouse for his or her lifetime and, upon the death of the surviving spouse, it would be distributed to the first deceased spouse's children.

In November, 2008, Wilma died. The figure below shows how the property was distributed pursuant to Wilma's Trust agreement.

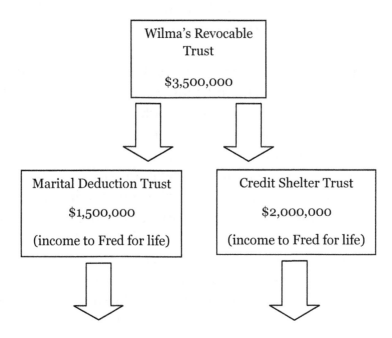

After Fred's death, all property in both
trusts distributed to Wilma's children

At Wilma's death, an amount equal to the full unified credit ($2,000,000) was distributed to the Credit Shelter Trust. This amount was held for Fred's benefit but did not become a part of Fred's estate. It passed into the Credit

Shelter Trust free of estate tax because it did not exceed the unified credit amount.

The remaining amount in Wilma's revocable Trust ($1,500,000) passed into the Marital Deduction Trust. There was no estate tax on this amount because it was a transfer to a surviving spouse and, because of the unlimited marital deduction, was not subject to estate taxes. It qualified for the marital deduction even though Fred could not touch the principal amount, because Fred was entitled to all of the income generated by the property in the Marital Deduction Trust.

During the remainder of his life, Fred received the income from both trusts and thus received the support that they both wanted. Upon Fred's death, the principal in both trusts passed to Wilma's children free of estate tax. The property in the Credit Shelter Trust was not taxed because it was not greater than the unified credit amount in effect at the time of Wilma's death. Even if the amount in the Credit Shelter Trust had increased to $10 million dollars, Wilma's children would have received it free of estate taxes. There would however, have been capital gains taxes due in that situation. The property in the Marital Deduction Trust passed to Wilma's children free of estate taxes because it became a part of Fred's estate and, combined with the value of the property Fred owned outright ($500,000), did not exceed the unified credit.

Because Fred and Wilma properly planned their estate, they were able to pass their assets to their children according to their wishes and without incurring any estate taxes. Let's see what would have happened had they not used trusts to plan their estates. We will assume that Fred and Wilma, as many couples do, had wills prepared that gave each of their estates to each other and after the death of the last one of them, $3.5 million to Wilma's children and $500,000 to Fred's children. If Wilma dies first, at her death all of her assets go to Fred. There is no estate tax because it is a transfer between spouses and the unlimited marital deduction is in effect. Fred, however, now has an estate valued at $4 million.

Upon his death (in 2008), Fred can pass $2 million to his and Wilma's children without estate taxes. The remaining $2 million is subject to estate taxes and Fred's estate will have to pay $1,005,000 in estate taxes. Because Fred and Wilma failed to set up a Credit Shelter Trust arrangement, they wasted Wilma's unified credit and their children lost almost a quarter of their inheritance.

Funding the Trust. The revocable Trust is a powerful and efficient estate planning tool to avoid probate and reduce estate taxes. However, it is important to understand that the Trust is only effective for those assets that have been transferred to the Trust. You can pay a fortune for a terrific Trust agreement, but if your assets are not titled in the name of the Trust, they will have to pass through probate to get to your heirs.

The first step in funding the Trust is determining the correct name to place your assets in. The property will not be owned by the Trust itself but by the Trustee subject to the terms of the Trust. In the above example, the proper way to designate ownership is:

Wilma Flintstone, Trustee of the Wilma Flintstone Trust dated July 4, 2000.

Any assets transferred to the Trust should be titled in this name. Deeds must be prepared to transfer real estate from the Grantor to the Trustee. If you remember from Chapter 3, transferring homestead to your Trust may create serious title problems. You should consult with a competent estate planning attorney before doing so. Bank accounts should be titled in the name of the Trustee, as should stocks, bonds and mutual funds. Individual retirement accounts, 401(k) plans, certain annuity contracts and other tax deferred investments will usually remain in the name of the Grantor. Transferring these investments into the Trust may have adverse tax consequences.

Regarding life insurance, you should consider having the wife own and be primary beneficiary of the insurance policy on the life of the husband and vice versa, and that the Trustee be named as a contingent beneficiary using the following designation: Successor Trustee of the Wilma Flintstone Trust dated July 4, 2000. You should contact your insurance agent and request him or her to provide you with the necessary forms to change ownership of the policies and to make the change of beneficiary as indicated.

Before naming the Trustee as beneficiary of any tax deferred investment, you should consult with your tax advisor. There may be advantages to naming individuals as beneficiaries as opposed to a trust.

Remember, if you do not transfer your assets to your Trust, it will do you no good in your goal to avoid probate. Any assets owned individually by you at the time of your death that do not have transfer on death or beneficiary designations will have to go through probate to get to your Trust and eventually to your heirs.

Pour-Over Wills. Even though you have prepared a Trust and transferred all of your assets into it, you still need a Will. No matter how careful and diligent you are in funding your Trust, it is always possible that you may forget to put an asset into it. It is also possible for you (your estate) to acquire property after your death such as an insurance settlement or an inheritance that you became entitled to during your lifetime but was not actually distributed until after the time of your death.

In these cases, the only way to get these assets to your heirs is through probate. A Pour-Over Will is similar to the Wills we discussed earlier; however, its purpose is to take any property not in your Trust at the time of your death and transfer or "pour it over" into the Trust. This requires the property to go through probate, so the Pour-Over Will is only used as a last resort or safety net. In the vast majority of well planned estates, it is never used.

Durable Power of Attorney. Another important tool in your estate plan is the Durable Power of Attorney. It is a document in which you appoint someone (usually your spouse, another family member or a close trusted friend) to act in your behalf and deal with and manage property which is not in the Trust if you are unable to do so yourself. This person is called your attorney-in-fact. The term "durable" shows your intent that the attorney-in-fact will have authority to act for you even if you are incapacitated. As we discussed earlier, IRAs are not transferred into the Trust. Therefore the Trustee has no authority over them. If you needed to take a distribution from your IRA and were incapacitated or otherwise unable to authorize such transaction, the attorney-in-fact named in your Durable Power of Attorney would be able to direct the distribution.

You may give the attorney-in-fact broad powers or limit his or her authority to specific tasks. It is also possible to set up the Power of Attorney so that it only becomes effective upon certain events such as written certification from a physician that you are unable to manage your own affairs.

This is called a "Springing Power of Attorney" because it only becomes valid or "springs" into action at the time of your incapacity.

The Durable Power of Attorney must be in writing and must also be signed by two witnesses. The attorney-in-fact may be a spouse, relative, friend or almost anyone you choose, provided that person is 18 or older and of sound mind. The Durable Power of Attorney is valid from the time you sign it until such time as you revoke it, you are declared incompetent by a court, or upon your death.

The importance of a Durable Power of Attorney becomes evident when you consider the alternatives. If you became incapacitated without a Durable Power of Attorney, a court would have to appoint a guardian to manage your affairs, pay your bills and maintain your property and investments. Guardianship proceedings can be time consuming and expensive and there is no guarantee that the court will appoint the person you would have wanted as guardian. You can easily avoid this situation if you plan and appoint an attorney- in-fact to act on your behalf.

With a well drafted Durable Power of Attorney, your attorney-in-fact will be able to "step into your shoes" and make decisions about your property. He or she would be able to sign checks to pay your bills and medical expenses, oversee and direct your investments, sign deeds and enter into contracts on your behalf. Of course you can structure the Durable Power of Attorney to restrict or eliminate any of these powers. That way you can provide for your incapacity without giving up control of your assets. Under no circumstance can an attorney-in-fact change your will, exercise personal services, or vote in any public election on your behalf.

Even if you have set up a revocable Trust, the Durable Power of Attorney is an important element of your estate planning. The primary reason most people set up trusts is to avoid probate; however, only assets that are properly transferred into trust ownership will escape probate administration. Therefore, if you become incapacitated and your family discovers that you forgot to transfer shares of stock into the Trust, those shares would be subject to probate at the time of your death. If you had executed a Durable Power of Attorney with specific authority to transfer assets to your Trust, your attorney-in-fact could put the stock into trust ownership prior to your death, thereby saving your heirs the time and expense of probate administration.

Conclusion. There is no "one size fits all" solution to estate planning. Every person has different objectives, assets and family circumstances. There are many ways to pass your estate to your heirs. Even a total absence of planning will result in the distribution of your estate. However, if you are concerned about avoiding probate, minimizing taxes, maintaining privacy and reducing administration costs, you must pro-actively plan your estate.

CHAPTER 6

Making Health Care
Decisions In Florida

The 2005 Terri Schiavo case thrust Florida into the forefront in the national debate about health care decision making and whether a person has a right to refuse medical care and treatment.

Terri Schiavo was a young woman who had a heart attack which severely damaged her brain, including her cerebral cortex which controls her conscious thought. Many doctors concluded that Terri's condition was a persistent vegetative state and she was institutionalized for 15 years until her death.

In 1988, her husband and court appointed guardian, Michael Schiavo, petitioned the Pinellas County Circuit Court to remove her feeding tube. He claimed that she had confided to him verbally that she would not want to be kept alive by artificial means. Terri's parents, Robert and Mary Schindler opposed this, saying that such a statement would be completely out of character for her and that she believed in the sanctity of life.

The court battle continued for 7 years and included 14 appeals in the Florida courts and 5 actions in Federal District Court. The Florida legislature passed a law, called "Terri's Law," which allowed Governor Jeb Bush to order her feeding tube reinserted. The Florida Supreme Court overturned the law and the United States Supreme Court four times refused to consider the case. Congress even tried to call for hearings on the matter under which they subpoenaed Terri and Michael Schiavo to testify.

Celebrities, politicians and advocacy groups publicly argued the issues of the case. The saga was played out on television and radio talk shows across the nation and it seemed everyone had an opinion about how Terri Schiavo should be treated medically.

Finally, on March 18, 2005, Circuit Court judge ordered Terri's feeding tube removed. After a flurry of last minute petitions and appeals, Terri Schiavo died on March 25, 2005, 15 years and one month after collapsing in her home. The debate still rages.

A sad but interesting fact is that all of this could have been avoided had Terri Schiavo made and executed a valid living will.

So, how can you, as a resident of Florida, make sure that you and your family don't fall into the same situation as the Schiavo and Schindler families? First, you must decide what your views and wishes are regarding your medical treatment. What are your guidelines for determining the type of treatment you wish to receive? Who do you want to make those decisions? Do you wish for heroic measures to be taken to keep you alive? Or do you wish for life prolonging procedures to be withdrawn? Second, you should put your wishes in writing in a proper legal form. And finally, you should discuss your wishes with your family and loved ones.

The right of a person in Florida to determine what medical treatment he or she will submit to is considered to be a constitutional right. In a 1990 decision, the Florida Supreme Court stated that "a competent person has the constitutional right to choose or refuse medical treatment, and that right extends to all relevant decisions concerning one's health."

The Florida legislature stated in its findings to Chapter 765 of the Florida Statutes (the Health Care Advance Directive Law), "that every competent adult has the fundamental right of self-determination regarding decisions pertaining to his or her own health, including the right to choose or refuse medical treatment." This is all well and good, but what happens if a person is incapacitated and cannot make his or her own health care decisions? The legislature specified, as an intent of the law, that a patient is allowed to plan for incapacity by designating another person to direct the course of medical treatment in the event of the patient's incapacity. This designation can be made in the form of a written document called an Advanced Directive.

The two types of Advanced Directives are the Designation of Health Care Surrogate and the Living Will.

Designation of Health Care Surrogate. Simply speaking, a Designation of Health Care Surrogate is a written document designating a person or surrogate to make health care decisions on your behalf. The document must be signed by the you (or you must direct someone to sign for you) in the presence of two separate witnesses who must also sign the document. The surrogate named in the document cannot serve as a witness.

The surrogate does not have any authority to make decisions on your behalf until it has been determined by your attending physician that you are physically or mentally unable to communicate a willful and knowing health care decision. This determination must then be corroborated by a second physician. If both physicians find that you cannot make health care decisions, they record that fact in your medical record and notify the surrogate in writing that he or she has authority to make the decisions.

Once the surrogate obtains authority to act, he or she is responsible to act for you and make all health care decisions during your incapacity in accordance with your instructions. The last phrase is why it is important that you carefully consider your wishes, put them in writing and discuss them with the surrogate and with your family.

Privacy Concerns. The properly drafted Designation of Health Care Surrogate allows the surrogate to consult with your doctors and health care providers in order to provide informed consent. When I say properly drafted, I mean that the document must address the federal Health Insurance Portability and Accountability Act (commonly known as HIPAA or the Privacy Act).

In 2003, Congress passed HIPAA to allow persons changing or terminating jobs to be able to keep health insurance coverage. Many of the regulations of HIPAA deal with the protection of the person's personal medical information. The law required all doctors, nurses, pharmacists and other health care providers to abide by these strict privacy rules or face penalties of fines or imprisonment. Because of this, health care providers have become reluctant to release patient's medical information to anyone, including spouses and children of the patient, unless that person is specifically authorized under the law to receive the information. Situations have arisen where a surrogate was authorized to make decisions on behalf of a patient but, because of HIPAA, did not have authority to obtain the information about the patient's condition necessary to make those decisions. It is important that you include language in your advance directives that specifically addresses the HIPAA issue and provides that your health care surrogate will be able to access the medical information they need.

Responsibilities of the Surrogate. After being authorized, the surrogate may consult with health care professionals, have access to your appropriate clinical records, apply for public benefits on your behalf, authorize release of information and records to appropriate persons and authorize your transfer and admission to and from a health care facility. Unless you expressly allow in writing, the surrogate may not consent to or authorize an abortion, sterilization, electroshock therapy, experimental treatments and voluntary admission to a mental health facility. The surrogate is also prohibited from withholding or withdrawing life-prolonging procedures from a pregnant patient, prior to the fetus' viability.

Whom to Appoint as Surrogate. The appointment of a health care surrogate is obviously an extremely important decision which can raise deep emotional issues. Most persons choose a family member or close friend whom they trust to make serious decisions. The person you choose as your surrogate should clearly understand your wishes regarding your health care and be willing to accept the responsibility of making medical decisions on your behalf. You may also consider your family's dynamics in making this decision. The situation when the surrogate will have to act will likely be a highly stressful and emotional experience for your family.

Some persons are better able to function in such a situation than others.

It is also a good idea to appoint a backup or alternate surrogate. The alternate can step in if your first selection for surrogate is unable, unwilling or unavailable.

You should keep your advance directive documents in a safe but accessible place at your home. These documents should not be stored in a safe deposit box as they may be needed immediately in an emergency and the bank may be closed at such time. You should also provide your doctor with a copy.

Living Will. A Living Will in Florida is a written declaration which states your intentions if you should be in a terminal condition, have an end-stage condition or are in a persistent vegetative state with no hope of recovery. Using this document you would direct whether you wanted life-prolonging procedures provided, withheld or withdrawn.

A "terminal condition" is defined under the Florida Statutes as a condition caused by injury, disease or illness from which there is no reasonable medical probability of recovery and which, without treatment, can be expected to cause death.

An "end-stage condition" means an irreversible condition that is caused by injury, disease or illness which has resulted in progressively severe and permanent deterioration, and which treatment, to a reasonable degree of medical probability, would be ineffective.

A "persistent vegetative state" is a permanent and irreversible condition of unconsciousness in which there is (a) the absence of voluntary action or cognitive behavior of any kind and (b) an inability to communicate or interact purposefully with the environment.

In determining your condition, your attending or treating physician and at least one other consulting physician must separately examine you. Both physicians must find that you suffer from one of the above conditions before life-prolonging procedures may be withheld or withdrawn.

A Living Will must be signed by you, or someone else at your direction, in the presence of two witnesses who must also sign the document. One of the witnesses has to be someone other than your spouse or blood relative. You may designate a surrogate to carry out your wishes, but the failure to do so will not make the Living Will invalid.

The law makes it your responsibility to notify your attending physician that the Living Will has been signed. For this reason, it is important that you bring the signed Living Will to your doctor as soon as possible after you have signed it. The doctor can make a copy to put into your medical records.

Procedure. If you have made a valid Living Will but have not designated a surrogate to execute your wishes contained in the Living Will, the physician may carry out the wishes as directed by the Living Will. If a family member or other person close to you objects to the withholding or withdrawing of life-prolonging procedures, the physician shall not withhold or withdraw until an expedited judicial review is made or until 7 days have passed if no review is sought.

Before proceeding, the physician or surrogate must be satisfied that: (a) you are incapacitated with no reasonable medical probability of recovery, (b) you are either in a terminal condition, end-stage condition or persistent vegetative state, and (c) any limitations or conditions expressed orally or in a written declaration have been carefully considered and satisfied.

If You Have No Living Will. If you have not prepared a living will, the person that have designated designated as a health care surrogate may make the decision to withhold or withdraw life-prolonging procedures. Before exercising such authority, the surrogate must be satisfied that you are incapacitated with no reasonable medical probability of recovery, and you are either in a terminal condition, end-stage condition or persistent vegetative state.

If you have not executed any advance directive, your health care decisions are then made by a proxy as determined by Florida law. The proxy is designated by law to be the following persons, in the order of priority set forth below.

(1) a judicially appointed guardian of you,

(2) your spouse,

(3) an adult child, or if more than one, a majority of the adult children who are reasonably available for consultation,

(4) a parent,

(5) an adult sibling, or if more than one, a majority of them,

(6) an adult relative who has exhibited special care and concern for you and who has maintained regular contact with you and is familiar with your activities, health and religious or moral beliefs, or

(7) a close friend.

However, as we saw in the Terri Schiavo case, there may be many other factors considered by the court in determining a proxy and in authorizing health care decisions.

Revocation or Amendment of an Advance Directive. You may amend or revoke a Designation of Health Care Surrogate or Living Will at any time, provided you are competent. The revocation can be made by a written instrument signed and dated by you, by the physical cancellation or destruction of the advance directive by you or by someone at your direction and in your presence, by your oral expression of intent to amend or revoke, or by your execution of a new advance directive that is different from the first.

Do Not Resuscitate Orders. A Living Will requires certain conditions regarding your conditions to exist before it can be used. If you are suffering from a chronic or terminal condition and have made a prior decision that you do not want to be resuscitated, there is another document that you should consider. A Do Not Resuscitate Order (or "DNR") is a written order from a doctor that, in the event you should suffer cardiac or respiratory arrest, you should not be resuscitated. DNR orders must typically be signed by two witnesses, you and also a doctor, yet the rules and requirements vary from hospital to hospital. It must be executed on Florida Department of Health and Rehabilitative Services Form 1896. If you are unable to sign the DNR, it may be signed by your health care surrogate, guardian or proxy, provided that such person determines that you have no reasonable probability of recovery and you would have made a similar decision.

Anatomical Gifts. Florida has adopted the Uniform Anatomical Gift Act. Any person who may make a Will may give all or part of his or her body upon death. The donor's intent may be expressed by a provision in his or her Will or by a separate document that is signed by the donor in the presence of two witnesses who must also sign the document in the presence of the Donor. The document may specify to whom the gift is being made, what parts of the donor's body are being gifted and any limitations upon the gift. If the document doesn't specify who will receive the gift, the gift may be accepted by the donor's attending physician following the donor's death.

The state of Florida has several programs in which anatomical gifts can be made. The Agency for Health Care Administration and the Department of Highway Safety and Motor Vehicles has a registry program which allows donors to make anatomical gifts by registration and notation on the donor's driver license or identification card.

As with any issues regarding health care and end of life decisions, you should discuss your wishes regarding anatomical gifts and organ donation with your family and loved ones.

CHAPTER 7

Buying A Home In Florida

There are many considerations to buying a home in Florida. You need to find an area that has the features you are looking for. You have to determine what price you can afford. Do you want to buy a newly constructed home or an existing one? Are you purchasing a part time home or will this be your primary residence?

Many of these issues are beyond the scope of this book. In this chapter, we are going to look at the process of buying the home once you have selected it. We will examine the advantages of using a real estate agent, what to look for when drawing up or reviewing a contract and what happens at the closing, among other issues.

Advantages of Using a Real Estate Agent. A real estate agent can help guide you through the buying process and provide you with information necessary to select a property and obtain financing. He or she can help you determine the purchase price you can afford and provide you with valuable information about the community.

After choosing the property, you should ask the agent to conduct a comparative market analysis to show you prices of other similar properties that have recently sold in the community. This, along with other factors can help you determine a proper offering price. The agent can then help you prepare a written offer and help you negotiate the final terms of the transaction.

Once a contract is entered into, a good agent will help you perform all of the items needed to facilitate the closing. These may include obtaining a survey, an appraisal, arranging for title insurance and other duties to help the transaction close smoothly. When interviewing an agent, make sure she is willing to provide these services to you.

In most situations, the agent is paid by the seller. When the seller lists the property with an agent, the seller agrees to pay that agent a commission if the property sells. If your agent was the cause of your introduction to the property the seller's agent splits the commission with your agent.

Selecting a Real Estate Agent. When selecting a real estate agent, it is important to know what his obligations are to you. Even though you have requested the agent to find properties for you and write the purchase offer, he may not legally be your agent. If he is also the listing agent for a property you are buying, he may have a duty to pass along confidential information you have given him to the seller.

In Florida, a real estate agent will either have a relationship with you as a "single agent" or a "transaction broker." A single agent represents either the buyer or the seller in a transaction, but cannot represent both. The single agent has a fiduciary relationship with his client, and owes the client the following duties: (1) dealing honestly and fairly, (2) loyalty, (3) confidentiality, (4) obedience, (5) full disclosure,

(6) accounting for all funds, (7) skill, care and diligence in the transaction, (8) presenting all offers and counteroffers in a timely manner, unless a party has previously directed the licensee otherwise in writing, and (9) disclosing all known facts that materially affect the value of residential real property and are not readily observable.

A single agent must disclose and describe his duties to you in writing prior to either entering into an agreement for representation or before showing any property, whichever occurs first.

A transaction broker provides limited representation to a buyer, a seller, or both in a real estate transaction, but does not represent either in a fiduciary capacity or as a single agent. The transaction broker has a duty of only limited confidentiality. This limited confidentiality, in the case of a buyer, prevents the agent from disclosing to you that the seller will accept a price less than the asking price. In the same way, the transaction broker cannot disclose to the seller that you, as the buyer, will pay a price greater than the one you submitted in a written offer. It also prevents the agent from disclosing either party's motivation for buying or selling, and any information that you or the seller has requested to remain confidential. Aside from these, the transaction broker may repeat conversations from you and the seller to the other party.

It is important to understand that, by using a transaction broker, you are giving up your rights to the undivided loyalty of the agent. The theory of this arrangement is that the agent can better facilitate a transaction by assisting both you and the seller, but cannot represent one party to the detriment of the other party.

In either situation, you should not assume that any real estate broker or agent represents you unless you agree to engage them in an authorized brokerage relationship, either as a single agent or a transaction broker. Do not disclose any information you want to be held in confidence until you have entered into an agreement with the agent. This includes the maximum purchase you are willing to pay and any time constraints you have.

The Contract. The most important document in any real estate transaction is the contract for sale and purchase. It is the blueprint of the transaction. All of the items you negotiated with the seller should be included in the contract.

Because of this, it is extremely important that the contract be drafted to clearly express the full intent of the buyer and seller. If a point you negotiated is left out of the contract, it is likely you will not be able to enforce that point.

Florida real estate transactions are subject to the Statute of Frauds which means that all agreements for the sale of real estate must be in writing. The writing does not have to be a formal contract. There are many cases where letters, notes, memoranda and other writings have formed an enforceable contract. However, to have a clear understanding of your intent and the intent of the seller, it is best to state the agreement in a single properly prepared contract.

Before we look at the specific provisions of a contract, you should have a basic understanding of some aspects of Florida contract laws.

A valid and enforceable agreement requires 3 things: an offer, acceptance of the offer and communication of that acceptance.

When one party to a transaction prepares a contract, signs it and presents it to the other party, an offer has been made. The other party then has three choices. She can accept the offer, reject the offer or make a counter offer.

Accept the Offer. If all of the terms of the offer are acceptable to the other party, she may accept the offer by signing it and communicating her acceptance to the offering party. This is usually done by providing the offering party, or his agent or attorney, the signed agreement. At this point there is a valid and binding agreement between the parties.

Reject the Offer. If the other party does not agree with all of the terms of the offer, she has two alternatives. She may reject the offer. This may be done by communicating to the offering party that the offer is rejected or by doing nothing.

Counter the Offer. The last alternative is to make a counter-offer. This occurs when the other party changes a provision or provisions of the offer and presents those changes to the offering party. In essence, you have now made an offer to the offering party.

If the offering party accepts these changes, we have an agreement. Otherwise, the offering party can make his counter-offer to the counter-offer or reject the changes. But until both parties agree to all of the terms, there is no contract.

Sometimes the changes are made on the face of the offer by crossing out items or handwriting provisions on the document. Other times a formal counter-offer document is presented to the offering party. Still other times the counter-offer is contained in a letter or other writing. However it is made, the writings must clearly show the intent of the parties.

Gathering Information. Before making or reviewing an offer, you, as a prospective purchaser, should have certain information. Much of the information is easily obtained and can be extremely valuable in structuring the transaction.

Property Information. The first thing you should do is look up the property on the county appraiser's website. You can find that site by doing a Google search on "Alachua County (or whatever county your property is located in) Property Appraiser." Most county appraiser's websites allow you to search for the property by address or owner's name. This listing can provide a lot of valuable information such as the owner's name, the parcel identification number of the property, the county appraiser's just valuation of the property, the taxable value of the property, whether the owner is receiving a homestead exemption, the legal description of the property, dates and purchase prices of past sales of the property, the amount and status of payment of property taxes and a description of improvements on the property.

Many appraiser's websites will provide a link to the county clerk's site to enable you to view a copy of the previous deed and search to determine whether the owner has a mortgage. All of this information can be valuable in negotiating the purchase price and other terms of the contract.

To help determine a purchase price, you should receive a market analysis from your real estate agent or an appraisal from a licensed appraiser. Generally, the fee for an appraisal is more than offset by the leverage it gives you in negotiating the purchase price.

Provisions of the Contract. Whether you are preparing an offer or reviewing an offer made by the other party, you should be familiar with certain provisions.

This section will take you step by step through a typical real estate contract. This is only an overview and should not take the place of the preparation or review of the contract by an attorney.

While we are on the topic of attorneys, please don't bring your contract to the attorney to review after you have already signed it. At that point, you have already agreed to the terms and making changes becomes much more difficult, if not impossible. Bring the offer you have received to the attorney so that, if necessary, she can prepare a counter-offer for you.

Better yet, have your attorney prepare the initial offer. This allows you to dictate the terms of the agreement. The seller will then be in the position of having to negotiate changes to the offer. Also, the seller may overlook some provisions which you have set up in your favor.

When reviewing or preparing an offer, you should create a separate checklist that you complete as you go through the document. The checklist should include, at a minimum, all contract deadlines, all expenses of the transaction and the responsible party, and any contingencies or special provisions. We will go through each of these in detail. A form of the checklist you can use may be found at www.newfloridaresident.com.

The Parties to the Contract. The sellers' names should appear exactly as they are on the deed in which they acquired title. If the property is jointly owned, all owners are required to be a party to the contract.

All persons named as sellers must sign the contract for it to be valid. If a property is owned by a husband and wife and only the husband signs the offer, it is not a valid offer and your response should be to require the wife to sign before responding to the terms of the offer.

If the property is owned individually by a married person and the house is his home, Florida homestead law requires the spouse to join in the transaction. You must add the name of the spouse and both must sign.

If the record owner of the property is deceased, the situation becomes a little more complicated. If the deceased owner's estate is in probate, the Personal Representative of the estate is usually the proper party. The seller's line should read, "John Smith, as the Personal Representative of the Estate of William Jones, deceased."

In this case you would have to determine whether the Personal Representative has authority to sell the property. First, he should produce "Letters of Administration" from the court which shows he has been appointed as personal representative.

In most cases a Personal Representative's authority is set forth in the Will. If not, approval of the sale by the probate court is necessary. If there is no Will or, if there is a Will but it does not give the Personal Representative authority, the sale should be made contingent on the authorization of the probate court. The contract should contain the provision, "this contract is conditioned on seller obtaining an order authorizing sale from the probate court."

If the property was the deceased person's homestead, you may need to acquire the signatures of all the heirs or beneficiaries under the will.

If the property is owned by a corporation, the seller's information should contain the exact name of the corporation and the contract should be signed by the president, vice president or other authorized agent or officer of the corporation. The website of the Florida Department of State (www.sunbiz.org) contains information on Florida corporations and limited liability companies.

If the property is owned by a Trustee, the deed where the Trustee acquires title should specify that the Trustee has authority to sell the property. If not, you or your attorney should review the trust document to make sure the Trustee actually has authority to sell the property. Also, in preparing the contract, the proper seller should be listed as the Trustee, not the trust entity.

If the seller is a non-resident alien, you may be responsible for withholding proceeds of the sale for payment of taxes under the provisions of the Foreign Investment in Real Property Tax Act (FIRPTA). A special FIRPTA provision should be included in the contract. Your real estate agent or attorney can provide this form.

Do not rely on information obtained from the property appraiser or the MLS listing. May times this information is incorrect or incomplete. To determine the proper sellers, you should always look to the previous deed.

You should be careful in the manner in which you take title. There is a discussion of the different alternatives at the end of this Chapter.

The address and phone number you put on the contract for each party should be accurate to make it easier for the closing agent to contact you. You should also specify somewhere in the contract the address where you want the property tax bill sent after you acquire ownership.

Legal Description. The contract should contain the legal description of the property. This can be an identification of a particular lot in a subdivision or a surveyor's description of the property. Again, you shouldn't rely on the county appraiser's information or the MLS description. Use the legal description from the prior deed. If the description is long, attach a copy of the deed as an exhibit.

You can add the property address and the parcel identification number to the legal description, but these should not be used in place of the legal description.

Purchase Price. The contract should clearly state the total purchase price you are paying for the property. It should also break down the manner that the purchase price will be paid.

Earnest Money Deposit. The buyer usually pays a deposit upon execution (or signing) of the contract. The deposit is intended to show that the buyer is entering into the contract in good faith. Forfeiture of the deposit is usually the seller's remedy if the buyer defaults.

You should specify an amount of the deposit and the name of the escrow agent who will hold the deposit. Always pay the deposit to an escrow agent, not to the seller. The escrow agent is typically either the real estate agent, closing agent, or your attorney. Also, I do not recommend giving the seller a "non-refundable" deposit. If the seller is unable to fulfill his obligations under the contract, you want to be able to get your deposit back.

Upon closing, the deposit will be applied toward the purchase price. Different aspects of the deposit and its disposition will be dealt with in other parts of this chapter.

Sometimes the deposit is paid in installments. If this is the case you should specify when the installment must be paid, and like the initial deposit, name an escrow agent. The due date of the installment should be noted on your contract deadline checklist.

Mortgages and Financing. You may wish to finance the purchase with a loan from a bank or from the seller. The amount of the loan should be specified and, if the seller is providing the financing, the terms of the mortgage should be spelled out.

If you are acquiring a mortgage from a bank, you should make your obligations under the contract contingent upon you acquiring the mortgage.

The contingency provision should state that if you are unable to acquire a certain mortgage within a specified number of days, you may cancel the contract and receive a full refund of your deposit. This date should be noted on your contract deadline checklist.

The contingency provision describes the type of mortgage you are seeking (fixed or adjustable), the highest interest rate you will accept and the term of years of the mortgage. It also sets forth the principal amount and fees that are acceptable to you.

The financing contingency requires that you act in good faith to attempt to acquire the mortgage. You must apply for the mortgage within a set number of days and diligently pursue the mortgage.

This means you must cooperate with the lender and provide the information it requires in a timely manner. If you fail to do this, the seller may declare the contract in default and seek a forfeiture of the deposit.

If you are unable to obtain a commitment from the lender within the number of days specified, you may inform the seller in writing of that fact, cancel the contract and receive a refund of your deposit.

You should note the date by which you are required to apply for the mortgage and the date by which you must notify the seller of your inability to obtain the mortgage on your contract deadline checklist.

Title Evidence. The contract should specify a date when the buyer is to receive a title insurance commitment. The cost of title insurance is generally a negotiated item, with either party being responsible or both parties sharing the cost. The person paying for title insurance should select the attorney or title company who will write the policy. Before making or accepting an offer, you should get a quote for title insurance as it is usually one of the major expenses of the transaction.

If you are obtaining a mortgage, the bank will require that you purchase title insurance to cover the bank's interest. This is generally a small sum added to the cost of the owner's title insurance. This is almost always an expense of the buyer.

Do You Need Title Insurance? Many buyers raise the question, "Do I really need title insurance? The Seller told me that he got title insurance when he purchased the property and hasn't had any liens on the property since. If that's true, why would I need title insurance?"

Title insurance affords protection to a purchaser for defects in the title not disclosed by a search of the public records, such as claims of undisclosed heirs, deeds by incompetent persons, forgeries, adverse possession and fraudulent statements of marital status in deeds. Even if the Seller had the title searched and can assure you that he kept the title clean, he would have no way of knowing about these defects. That is what title insurance covers. If a defect is found, the title insurance company would pay the cost of clearing the title or would refund your purchase price.

If you purchase title insurance at the closing, the attorney or title company will conduct a search of the county's public records to determine whether the seller actually owns the property and whether there are any encumbrances such as liens, easements or options affecting the property. If the search reveals that the seller does not actually own the property or that there are defects in the title, such as liens, and these conditions cannot be corrected, you can cancel the contract and receive a full refund of your deposit.

Prior to the closing, you will receive a title insurance commitment which insures the marketability of the title to the property subject to any exceptions specifically listed in such commitment. Your attorney could then advise you of the effect the exceptions have on the title and whether they are acceptable. After the deed is recorded, the search of the records is updated and you are issued a final title insurance policy. If it is later determined that a defect exists affecting the marketability of the title to your property, and the defect is not listed as an exception in the policy, you are insured up to your purchase price. The insurer is also obligated to pay the costs, attorneys' fees and expenses incurred defending the title to the property.

The cost of title insurance is a one-time charge typically paid at closing. An owner's policy for a $100,000 purchase usually costs about $700 and can be paid by the seller, the buyer or split between them. In transactions involving mortgage financing, the lender will always require the buyer to purchase title insurance protecting its loan. The attorney or title insurance agent can issue the lender's policy simultaneously with the owner's policy at little additional cost.

Other Expenses. Most contract forms have a provision that allocates the responsibility for payment of various expenses of the transaction. The parties are always free to negotiate these costs but custom usually prevails.

The largest expense is the documentary stamp tax on the deed. This is basically a transfer tax on the transaction and is customarily paid by the seller.

The amount of the documentary stamp tax on the deed is equal to seventy cents ($0.70) for every hundred dollars of the purchase price. For example, if the purchase price is $300,000, then the documentary stamp tax will be $2,100.

The buyer is usually responsible for the costs of recording the deed and any financing documents such as the mortgage. The recording cost for each document is $10.00 for the first page and $8.50 for each additional page.

The buyer is also customarily responsible for the expenses related to the financing of the transaction. These costs include documentary stamp tax on the amount of the loan ($0.35 for every $100) and an intangible tax on the mortgage (total amount of the loan multiplied by .002).

As previously stated, the buyer will pay any expenses related to the lender's title insurance coverage.

Prorations and Credits. Certain expenses such as property taxes and condominium or homeowner association assessments are prorated through the day prior to the closing date.

In Florida, property taxes for the calendar year are billed in arrears in November. This means that the November, 2008, tax bill covers the period of time from January 1, 2008, through December 31, 2008.

If the closing occurs prior to November, the property taxes will not have been billed or paid. In this case, you as the buyer, will receive the tax bill in November and pay the entire amount. You will be credited at closing for the share of the taxes representing the time period that the seller owned the property.

In this situation, the actual amount of property taxes is not known since they have not been billed. The proration will be estimated based on the previous year's taxes.

If you close on a purchase prior to November, you should make sure there is a provision for reproration of the taxes. This allows you to recalculate the proration amounts after the tax bill comes out and obligates the seller to reimburse you for any shortfall.

For condominium and homeowners associations, you should get a letter specifying the amount of the assessments and whether the seller is current in paying them. These fees can then be prorated based on this information. Some associations also require you to be approved to purchase the property. This usually requires payment of an application fee. Also, the certificate of approval may need to be recorded in the public records.

The Closing.   This section of the contract defines the closing date and the place of closing. You should choose a date that is convenient to you and, if you are financing the purchase with a loan, allow enough time for the lender to approve and process the loan.

If you are paying for the title insurance, you should demand that the closing occur at your attorney's office or title company that is writing the title insurance.

Inspection and Repair. More disputes and lawsuits are based on this provision than any other in the contract.

First of all, you should strongly consider hiring a licensed property inspector to inspect the property. An inspector can find items related to the condition of the property that a layperson would miss.

The best possible scenario is to add a provision to the contract making your obligations contingent upon your approval of the condition of the house based on the inspection. If for any reason specified in the inspection report you are not satisfied with the condition of the property, you can cancel the contract and receive a full refund of your deposit.

Many times the seller will not agree to this and will insist upon relying on the standard provision in the contract. If this is the case, you must read this provision carefully. It usually provides that the seller is warranting only structural items and not cosmetic items. Any time periods set forth for inspection and providing notice should be noted on your contract deadline checklist.

Many contract forms provide that a seller must pay a specified amount or percentage of the purchase price towards repairs. If the estimated cost of repairs exceeds this amount, either party may cancel the contract and the buyer's deposits are refunded or the transaction can continue and you will be responsible for the cost of all repairs exceeding the specified amount.

Occupancy. The contract should provide that you will take occupancy at the closing date. Do not let the seller, seller's tenant or any other person retain occupancy after closing unless you have an agreement addressing payment of costs, liability for damage and a set termination date for their occupancy. I would strongly recommend a formal lease agreement in this case, complete with payment of first and last month's rent and security deposit. This might seem a little extreme to you; however, I have seen situations like this turn into nightmare experiences for the new owner.

"As-Is." Many sellers insist on not giving any warranties relating to the condition of the property. Under an "as is" clause, you would purchase the property at the condition it is in at the effective date of the contract. If there are defects in the condition of the property, you have agreed to accept them.

The seller still has a responsibility to maintain the condition existing as of the date of the contract until the closing.

If you are contemplating entering into a contract with an "as is" clause, you should make sure it provides an inspection period and allows you to cancel the contract for any reason during the inspection period. Since you will not have any recourse for defects, it is important that you have the property professionally inspected.

Survey. Most contracts provide that the buyer has the right to obtain a survey at his own expense. The survey shows the boundaries of the property and the location of the improvements constructed on the property. It shows whether improvements from other parcels encroach onto the property or if any improvements built on the property encroach on other parcels or violate setback restrictions. The survey will set forth the size of the property, easements on the property and whether the property has access to a public road.

It is always advisable to have a current survey of the property. If you are financing the purchase with a mortgage, the lender will require a survey.

Time of the Essence. When a contract states that "time is of the essence," it means that all deadlines set forth in the contract will be strictly enforced. For this reason it is important to create a contract deadline checklist and make sure you comply with it.

The Closing. After you have entered into the contract, completed your inspections and acquired your funds, the day will come for you to take ownership of the property.

This process is called the "Closing." The Closing is the point of time when title to the property transfers from the seller to you.

At the closing, you and the seller will be required to execute certain documents to complete the transaction. A description of the main documents follows below:

Deed. The purpose of the deed is to convey title to the property. There are a number of different types of deeds, but as a purchaser, you should seek a warranty deed.

In a warranty deed, the seller warrants good title to the property and agrees to defend the title against any lawful claims against it. This means the seller agrees to be liable for any liens or other title problems arising before the Closing.

If the seller is not giving full warranties with respect to the title, other types of deeds such as a special warranty deed will be used.

If the seller is giving no warranties as to the title and is basically saying, "whatever interest I have in the property (even if it is none), I am conveying to you," he will use a quit claim deed.

Deeds must be signed by all sellers who have an ownership interest in the property and each seller's signature must be witnessed by two witnesses. The seller's signature should also be acknowledged by a notary. The deed should be made of public record by recording it in the office of the clerk of the circuit court in the county where the property is located. When reviewing the deed, you should make sure that you are receiving title in the manner you prefer. The correct parties should be named and spelled correctly. The address stated for you is the address to which the tax bill will be sent.

Bill of Sale. If personal property, such as furniture and appliances, is included in the transaction, it will be conveyed by a bill of sale. The bill of sale should be signed by the seller and contain a detailed description of the personal property conveyed.

Closing Statement. For those of you who like to "follow the money," the closing statement will be your favorite document. The closing statement, or settlement statement, is an accounting of the transaction. It sets forth the charges and credits to the buyer and seller and culminates, for the buyer, with the amount of cash needed at closing to pay the purchase price and the costs and expenses of the transaction attributed to the buyer.

The most common form of closing statement is the HUD-1 Settlement Statement which is required to be used when the transaction contains a government insured loan. Many closing agents use this form even when there is a conventional loan or cash deal.

The closing statement is divided into two columns, one for the seller and one for the buyer. Each column shows that party's share of the costs and expenses of the transaction as well as other charges and credits. It is important to point out that the allocation of costs and expenses shown on the closing statement is determined by the terms of the contract.

Let's take a look at the buyer's side of the closing statement. First of all, the buyer is always referred to as the borrower on a HUD-1 Settlement Statement, whether there is a loan or not.

The first section lists the charges to the buyer or the amounts the buyer is required to pay. This begins with the purchase price. The purchase price should be stated as the total purchase price set forth in the contract. Other charges to the buyer include the part of the purchase price allocated to personal property and pro-rated charges that the seller has already paid which the buyer will be reimbursing at Closing.

An example of these pro-rated charges is the real estate property tax. In Florida, the period for which property taxes are based is the calendar year. Taxes are paid in arrears. When the tax bill is sent in November, 2009, it covers the taxes for the period beginning January 1, 2009 and ending December 31, 2009.

If the closing occurs after November 1, and the seller has paid the property taxes, the buyer is charged an amount equal to the prorated share of taxes allocated to the period beginning on the closing date and ending December 31. The seller receives a credit for the same amount.

If the closing takes place before the property taxes are billed, the procedure is reversed. The buyer receives a credit for the pro-rated share of property taxes allocated to the period beginning January 1 and ending on the date of closing. The seller has a corresponding charge of the same amount.

Then when the property taxes are billed, the buyer is responsible for paying the entire bill. Keep in mind that the buyer had received a credit at closing for the period of time that the seller owned the property. Also, if the seller obtained the homestead exemption for the year of the transaction, you will get the benefit of the reduced taxes for that year.

If the pro-rations are made before the taxes are billed, the actual amount of taxes for the year in which the closing is held is unknown. In that case, the closing agent estimates the total taxes based on the previous year's amount. Since the actual taxes may be different from the previous year, every closing occurring prior to November should include a tax re-proration agreement.

Under a tax re-proration agreement, the buyer and seller agree that when the tax bill comes out in November, they will pro-rate the taxes based on the actual amount. If the charges and credits are different from those based on the estimated numbers, the parties will reimburse each other.

Other expenses that are pro-rated similar to property taxes are condominium or homeowners association assessments, rents received from tenants of the property, and insurance premiums.

Line 103 is the total of the buyer's settlement costs. It is the total amount of all expenses listed on the buyer's side of the second page.

The settlement charges fall under the following categories:

Real Estate Broker's Commission. This expense is based on the purchase price and is generally paid by the seller.

Loan Expenses. These are costs associated with your loan. They include origination fees, points, discount fees, appraisal fee, tax service fee and other fees negotiated between your lender and you.

These fees must be disclosed and estimated at the time you apply for the loan. That is the time to question or negotiate the fees, not at the Closing.

Items Required by Lender to be Paid in Advance. These include insurance premiums for hazard and, if applicable, flood insurance.

It also includes pre-paid interest. If the closing date is March 5, the first loan payment will usually be due on May 1. This payment includes a portion of the principal together with the interest accrued between April 1 and April 30. The interest accrued between March 5 and March 31 is payable in advance at the Closing and is shown on the Settlement Statement.

Reserves. In many loans, the lender will pay certain expenses such as insurance premiums and property taxes out of an escrow fund each year over the life of the loan. The reserve amounts are calculated each year and one-twelfth of the reserve is paid with each month's loan payment. When the expenses come due, such as property taxes in November, the lender pays them out of the escrow account.

The amount of reserves on the settlement statement includes the sums necessary to bring the escrow account current together with a predetermined cushion. For example, if your Closing took place in May, the lender would require reserves paid at the Closing for the portion of property taxes representing the months prior to and including May. In this manner, there will be enough funds in the escrow account to pay the taxes as they are billed in November.

If, for some reason (increase in property tax rates, increase in insurance premiums) the amount in the escrow account is not sufficient to pay the expenses, the lender will usually pay the difference and give you the option of paying them back in a lump sum or monthly installments over the next year.

Title Charges. This is the cost of title insurance. As mentioned earlier, payment of the title insurance cost for the owner's title insurance policy is negotiated between you and the seller. The buyer almost always pays the cost of the lender's coverage. Generally, this is a small fee called a simultaneous issue charge (since the lender's policy is being issued simultaneously with the owner's policy).

Many times the lender will require certain endorsements to its title insurance coverage. The expense of these endorsements is usually borne by the buyer.

Title charges also include a settlement or closing fee to the closing agent and expenses of the search of the title.

Recording Costs. The buyer is usually responsible for the costs of recording the deed and the mortgage. The seller traditionally pays the documentary stamp tax associated with the deed and the buyer pays the documentary stamp tax on the note and the intangible tax on the mortgage. Recording fees for each document are generally $10.00 for the first page and $8.50 for each additional page.

The documentary stamp tax on the promissory note is calculated by multiplying $0.35 by each hundred dollars of the loan. For example, if the loan amount is $100,000, the documentary stamp tax would be $100,000 □ 100 = $1,000 x 0.35 = $350.00.

The intangible tax on the mortgage is calculated by multiplying the amount of the loan by .002. The intangible tax on a $100,000 loan would be $100,000 x .002 = $200.00.

Additional Settlement Charges. These expenses include survey fees, pest inspection costs and postage and delivery. Usually, a lender will require the loan documents to be sent to it by overnight mail after the buyer signs. This cost is borne by the buyer.

Also, if loan funds are wired to the closing agent, the buyer pays the wiring fees.

The total of all of the settlement charges on the second page is shown in line 103 on the first page.

Line 120 is the gross amount due from the buyer or the total of all the debits of the buyer.

The format of the settlement statement is to calculate the total amount owed by the buyer (purchase price, closing costs, taxes) and subtract from it the total amount credited to the buyer to determine the amount of cash the buyer needs to bring to the Closing.

The bottom half of the first page lists the amounts that have been paid by or on behalf of the buyer. These are the items credited to the buyer.

The first item already paid by the buyer is the deposit or earnest money paid at the time the contract was signed and any additional deposits paid by the buyer.

If the buyer is financing the transaction with a loan and mortgage, the total principal amount is credited to the buyer since this is an amount the buyer will not have to pay at the Closing. The lender pays that part of the purchase price on the buyer's behalf.

If the seller has not paid the property taxes, the buyer will get a credit for the pro-rated amount allocated to the period of time the seller owned the property.

The total of all amounts paid by or on behalf of the buyer is shown on line 220. It is subtracted from the gross amount due from the buyer listed on line 120 to determine the amount due from the buyer at closing. If this amount is a negative number, it means the buyer will receive money at closing.

You should carefully review the settlement statement to make sure your name is correct and that the allocation of expenses match what was agreed to in the contract. If there are items you do not understand or that you disagree with, ask your attorney or the closing agent to explain them.

Promissory Note. If you are financing your purchase with a loan, the promissory note or note is the written evidence of the debt.

The note will name the buyer as the borrower. If persons other than those who will take title to the property are assuming liability for payment of the loan, it should be stated on the note.

The name of the lender is set forth on the face of the note. The lender may be a bank or other institution or it may be the seller. If the seller finances a part of the purchase price, the terms of the loan will be set forth in the contract. You should carefully review the note to make sure its terms comply with those in the contract.

The note will state the total principal amount of the loan and provide a period of time or term by which the loan must be paid in full.

The note also specifies the interest rate. This is the cost to you of the funds you borrowed to purchase the property. The interest rate is stated as a percentage and is the percentage of the loan balance that you pay each year.

For example, if the principal amount of the loan is $100,000 and the interest rate is 6% per annum (per year), the borrower will pay $6,000 per year in interest.

The interest rate can be fixed, which means it is the same throughout the life of the loan, or adjustable, which means it changes at certain times based on certain factors.

If a loan is a one-year adjustable rate loan, the interest rate will change, or adjust, each year on the anniversary date of the loan. The new interest rate is determined by taking a base rate (an interest rate such as the prime lending rate which is published) and adding to it a margin amount (a pre-specified rate set forth as a percentage in the note). The new interest rate will be applied against the outstanding principal until the next anniversary date at which time the rate is recalculated.

Adjustable rate mortgages carry a lot of risk since they can increase and cause a corresponding increase in payments. For this reason the initial interest rate for adjustable rate loans are typically lower than those of fixed rate loans.

Most loans are amortized. This means that each equal monthly payment contains a part of the principal of the loan together with the interest attributed to the outstanding principal for that month. The payments are structured such that the last of the principal is paid on the last payment.

Each month the outstanding principal of the loan is decreased. As a result, the interest payment is based on a smaller amount of principal each month and is also smaller. Since the dollar amount of each payment remains the same, more of the payment is applied toward the principal each month and the loan is gradually paid off.

Instead of being amortized, some loans call for the payment of interest only with the principal being paid at specified times or in a lump sum.

If the note provides that all of the remaining principal be paid at once, this is called a balloon payment. Many loans held by sellers are structured with balloon payments due after a number of years. The intent is that, by the time the balloon payment is due, the buyer can refinance the loan with a bank or other lender.

An important aspect for a borrower is the right to prepay the loan without penalty. Some notes provide that, if the borrower pays all or part of the principal balance on the note before it is due, the borrower must pay an additional amount (prepayment penalty) to compensate the lender for the interest it would not receive. You should carefully review the note to determine whether it contains a prepayment penalty.

Most notes provide for a late fee for any payments that are not made in a timely manner. Most provide for an additional amount of 5% of the amount of the payment due if the payment is more than 10 days past due.

If payment is not made, after a certain period specified in the note, the lender may accelerate the payments due under the note. This means it may declare the entire outstanding principal together with all accrued interest immediately due and payable in full.

Finally, many promissory notes have a "due on sale" clause. This provision prohibits the buyer (borrower) from transferring any interest in the property to another person. This includes adding someone's name on the title to the property. If the buyer does transfer any interest, the lender has the remedy of accelerating the payments.

Mortgage. Now that you have signed the note and owe the lender all that money, the lender wants some assurance that you will pay the loan. By executing the mortgage, you grant to the lender a lien against your property to secure the payment of the note.

The mortgage is recorded in the public records of the county where the property is located to put the public on notice of the lien.

It is important to understand that, in Florida, the mortgage does not transfer title to the property to the lender. Many times you will hear someone answer the question, "Do you own your own home?" with, "yes, me and the bank." While this answer indicates that he has a mortgage, it is not entirely accurate.

What the bank has is a lien against the property - the right to foreclose if the borrower defaults in the payment of the note or in the performance of certain conditions and obligations set forth in the mortgage.

Some of these conditions and obligations are:

1. Payment of the principal, interest and other sums required by the note and mortgage as they become due.
2. Payment of all taxes, assessments and other obligations affecting the property within the time provided by law.
3. Obtaining and maintaining casualty and, if applicable, flood insurance with coverage in an amount needed to protect the lender's interest in the loan.
4. Keeping the property in good condition and not doing any alteration, demolition or other action that would negatively affect the value of the property.
5. Compliance with all terms, conditions and agreements of the note and mortgage.

If the borrower does not perform any of these conditions or obligations, it will be considered an event of default.

If an event of default occurs and continues after notice from the lender, the lender generally has the following remedies:

1. Accelerate the amounts due under the note and declare the unpaid principal and accrued interest immediately due and payable.
2. Sue the borrower to obtain a foreclosure judgment in the amount of the unpaid principal, all accrued interest, and any expenses incurred to enforce the note and mortgage, including attorneys' fees and court costs.
3. If the lender obtains a judgment, it may have the court order the property sold at public judicial sale. Any proceeds from the sale will be applied against

the amount of the judgment. If the purchase price at judicial sale is less than the amount of the judgment, the borrower may be liable for the difference (or deficiency).

Once the mortgage is paid in full by the borrower, the lender executes a Satisfaction of Mortgage and records it in the public records. This removes the lien from the property.

At the Closing, the mortgage must be signed by anyone who has an ownership interest in the property, whether their name is on the note or not. If the property encumbered by the mortgage is homestead property, both husband and wife must execute the mortgage. This is true even if one of them is not named in the deed as an owner. See the previous Chapter on Homestead.

Buyer's Affidavit. This document is the buyer's representation under oath that the buyer knows of no claims that may be secured by a lien on the property, such as judgments or tax deficiencies against the buyer. If the buyer has a judgment against him, it may become a lien against the property when he acquires title. These representations are relied on by the title insurance underwriter in issuing both the owner's and mortgagee's policy.

The seller is usually required to sign a similar affidavit to give assurance to the buyer and title insurance underwriter that there are no liens against the property that have not been disclosed in the public records.

Survey. If there is a lender involved, the buyer is generally responsible for furnishing a survey prepared by a licensed professional land surveyor. The survey specifies the boundaries of the property, shows whether any improvements encroach upon the boundaries or easements and sometimes shows the elevation of and access to the property.

If there have not been any improvements constructed on the property since the date of the last survey, a copy of such last survey together with an affidavit from the seller stating that there have been no improvements constructed will suffice to meet the survey requirements of the contract.

The survey is required in order to delete the survey exception from the final title insurance policy.

Executing the Documents. Whether certain documents are valid and enforceable is dependent on proper execution of those documents. For example, two persons are required to witness the signatures of all of the sellers on the deed. All documents that are to be recorded in the public records must be notarized.

If you have documents that must be witnessed, you should follow these instructions: Two persons, one of whom may be the notary public who will acknowledge the signing, are required to witness the signatures of all parties who have signed the document. Each witness must be present when the instrument is signed. Each witness should print his or her name below the signature.

If a document is required to be notarized, you must appear personally before a notary public and sign the document where indicated. You then should acknowledge the execution of the document by stating to the notary, "I acknowledge I signed this document."

The notary will then complete the acknowledgment form by inserting the state and county where you executed the document, the date of execution and the notary's commission number and expiration date. The notary should then affix a notary seal.

No changes should be made to the documents without approval of the preparer.

Reviewing the Title Insurance Commitment. Before closing, you should receive a title insurance commitment from the closing agent. This document shows the instruments recorded in the public records that affect the title to the property. It lists all of those instruments. These are exceptions to the title. Since you have been put on notice that these instruments exist and that they affect title to the property you are going to purchase, the title insurance will not cover you for losses resulting from these instruments. A large part of your review of the commitment is to determine whether the instruments set forth in the commitment are acceptable to you.

For example, an easement along the side of the property for utility lines may be acceptable, while a lien for non-payment of construction costs will not.

The title commitment is divided into two sections, Schedule A and Schedule B. Schedule B has two parts to it, Schedule B-1 and Schedule B-2.

The top of Schedule A states the effective date of the commitment. This is the date to which the public records were searched. Most counties' public records access lags a few days behind. As a result the effective date will usually be earlier than the date of closing. As a result, the title insurance underwriter will provide "gap" coverage, insuring the period of time from the effective date to the closing date.

Schedule A then names the persons being insured: you as the purchaser and, if there will be a mortgage, the lender. You should review this provision to make sure your name is properly spelled and displayed exactly as it will be on the deed. The coverage amount, which for the owner is the purchase price and for the lender is the loan amount, is also listed.

The legal description of the property and the current owners of the property are also listed on Schedule A.

Schedule B-I lists the things that must be done at closing to effectively transfer marketable title to you. The execution, delivery and recording of the deed is always listed. If there are documents required to clear the title, such as satisfaction of the seller's mortgage, the execution and recording of those documents is listed. The documents may include affidavits needed to clear title, payment of property taxes and liens and corrective deeds. At closing, you should have the title insurance agent indicate in writing on the commitment that the items in Schedule B-1 have been complied with.

If you are financing the purchase with a loan, the execution, delivery and recording of the mortgage will also be included in Schedule B-1.

Schedule B-2 lists all instruments appearing in the public records that are an encumbrance or otherwise adversely affect title to the property. These may include liens, deed restrictions, agreements affecting the title or use of the property and easements. The title insurance underwriter will not cover you for items listed under Schedule B-2.

You should have your attorney review Schedule B-2 to make sure none of the items will cause problems for you.

Schedule B-2 includes the standard exceptions that are generally listed on the inside of the commitment cover. They include property taxes for the year indicated in the effective date unless the closing occurs between November 1 and December 31 of such year and proof of payment is obtained. If these requirements are met, the tax exception is waived and deleted from the commitment and you will be covered for any property taxes due prior to the Closing and not paid.

The standard exceptions also exclude from coverage damages resulting from persons such as tenants or guests in possession of the property, encroachments of buildings over boundary lines or easements and potential construction liens that have not yet been filed against the property.

These exceptions may be removed by an accurate survey and the owner's affidavit. This is why you may want to have a survey prepared for the property. In most cases you wouldn't be able to tell whether your neighbor's driveway or fence is on your property without a survey. If the survey and affidavits show no problems, you should request that the title agent remove those from the standard exceptions.

Winding Up. Before leaving the Closing, you should receive copies of all of the documents you have signed, a copy of the executed deed and owner's affidavit, the original signed bill of sale and the title commitment.

The closing agent is responsible for recording the deed, mortgage and other applicable documents in the public records. Within a few weeks you should receive from the closing agent the original recorded deed and the final owner's title insurance policy.

Immediately after closing, you should contact all utility companies and have the accounts transferred into your name. Some companies may require a copy of the deed as proof of your ownership.

Keep the documents in a safe place. The owner's title insurance policy and owner's affidavit will be necessary if a problem with the title to the property is ever discovered.

Alternatives for Taking Title

You should carefully consider how you will take title to the property. If you and your spouse are purchasing the property, you have the alternative of owning it as "tenants by the entireties." **Tenancy by the Entireties** is an ownership available only to husband and wife. It provides a right of survivorship which means, if one spouse dies the surviving spouse is the sole owner of the property. The property does not have to go through probate. While both spouses own the property the consent of both is needed to sell or place a lien on the property.

If you are purchasing the property with one or more other persons, you have two alternatives.

Under **Joint Tenancy with Right of Survivorship** you and the other owners have equal ownership interests in the property. Upon the death of one of the joint tenant owners, the remaining owners will have equal ownership of the property. Again there is no need for probate. All owners must consent to the sale or mortgaging of the property. See the Joint Ownership section of Chapter 5 for a more complete discussion of the pros and cons of owning a property as joint tenants with right of survivorship.

If you wish for the owners to have unequal shares or if you do not want a right of survivorship, then two or more persons can own a property as **Tenants in Common**. Under tenancy in common all owners are required to consent to the sale or mortgage of the property. However, if one of the joint tenants dies, his share is subject to probate and is distributed according to the terms of his Will, or if he has no Will, the Florida laws of intestate succession.

CHAPTER 8

Buying A Condominium in Florida

Condominium ownership is perfect for part-time residents of Florida. You don't have to worry about the upkeep and repair of a big house. There is absolutely no yard work and you'll have a pool, tennis court and clubhouse.

However, a condominium is a completely different animal than what you've been used to. It all starts with the ownership concept. First of all, most people refer to the apartment in which they will be living as their "condominium." Actually, the condominium is the entire project consisting of all of the apartments, the grounds, the parking areas and, in most cases, the recreational facilities. Your apartment is referred to as a "unit." All the rest of the condominium is known as the "common elements." You have exclusive ownership of your unit and you share in the ownership of the common elements with all of the other unit owners. The law says that all of you have an undivided ownership in the common elements. This means every unit owner has the right to enjoy the common elements and the obligation to maintain them.

As you may guess, this arrangement, without guidelines and management, could lead to utter chaos. Each unit owner would assert his or her own personal and selfish preferences as to the use of the common elements and many would not want to pay their fair share of the expenses.

That is where the condominium association comes in. The association is a non-profit corporation which is responsible for the operation and management of the condominium. Every unit owner is a member of the association. The unit owners elect a board of directors who in turn elect officers (president, secretary, treasurer, etc.). The board of directors has the authority to run the association and the officers are authorized to act on behalf of the board.

Because of the close proximity to your neighbors, the need to regulate the use of the common elements and the necessity of insuring, maintaining and repairing the common elements, certain rules and restrictions must exist. These rules and restrictions are found in the condominium documents. Although we will look at each document in more detail later in this chapter, a brief list of the documents is as follows:

1. Declaration of Condominium. This is the main document of the condominium. The Declaration actually creates the condominium. It describes the units and common elements, defines certain unit owner rights, authorizes creation of the association and regulates the use and operation of the common elements.

2. Articles of Incorporation of the Association. This document creates the condominium association. It is filed with the Florida Department of State.

3. Bylaws of the Association. These are the guidelines for the operation of the association. The bylaws set forth the number of directors, prescribes the procedures of unit owner and board of directors meetings and defines the financial and budget matters of the association.

4. Operating Budget. This document describes the common expenses of the association, which are divided among the unit owners in the same proportion as the ownership interest in the common elements.

5. Rules and Regulations. These are enacted by the board of directors and generally consist of restrictions pertaining to the use of the common elements.

The expenses involved in the operation of the association and the maintenance and repair of the common elements are shared by the unit owners in the same proportion as their ownership of the common elements.

The budget is determined by the board of directors and the unit owners pay monthly, quarterly or annual assessments. The payment of these assessments is secured by a lien on the condominium unit. If the unit owner fails to pay the assessments, the association may file a claim of lien in the county public records and, if necessary, foreclose on the lien.

In addition to the regular assessments based on the budget, the association may levy special assessments to cover unanticipated expenses such as repairs.

Unless waived by a majority of the unit owners, the association is required to create and maintain reserve accounts for large future expenses. The funds may be set up to cover such items as roof replacement, repaving of roads and parking areas, repainting buildings and repair and refurbishment of recreational areas. The funds are added to each year with the expectation that enough money will be available when the need arises.

Purchasing a Condominium Unit. If you have decided that condominium life is right for you, you may wish to purchase a unit. The purchase of a condominium unit involves many of the same considerations we discussed in Chapter 7. However, because of the unique nature of condominiums, there are other factors to consider.

There are two circumstances in purchasing a condominium unit which are treated differently under the law. There are different requirements depending on whether you are purchasing from a developer or from the prior unit owner.

Purchasing from a Developer. If you are purchasing a unit in a new project from the developer, the Florida condominium law has provisions to make sure you are informed. Every developer of a residential condominium is required to submit the condominium documents to the Division of Florida Land Sales, Condominiums, and Mobile Homes for review. The developer may not enter into contracts for the purchase and sale of a unit until it has submitted these documents and the Division has acknowledged that the documents were property submitted.

Reservation Program. However, prior to the submission of these documents, the developer may enter into reservation agreements with purchasers and accept reservation deposits. Many developers do this to create interest in a project and to see how well it will sell. By entering into a reservation agreement, you reserve your right to enter into a contract to purchase a certain unit in the condominium. You may cancel your reservation and receive a full refund of your deposit at any time and for any reason. The developer may also decide not the build the project, in which case it must promptly refund your deposit.

After the division has acknowledged that the condominium documents were properly submitted, the developer may enter into binding contracts for the sale of units. At this time the developer may ask you to enter into a contract to purchase your unit and transfer the reservation deposit into a sales deposit.

Buying the Unit. The developer will present you with a purchase contract and a set of disclosure documents. From the date you sign the contract or from the date you receive the disclosure documents, whichever is later, you will have 15 days to rescind the contract. If for any reason during those 15 days you decide you do not wish to purchase the unit, you may inform the developer in writing and the contract will be cancelled and your deposit fully refunded. This period is designed to provide you with an opportunity to review the disclosure documents.

When you receive the disclosure documents, the developer will ask you to sign a receipt for the condominium documents. This is a form required by the division to verify on which date you received the disclosure documents. You should make sure that you have actually received all of the documents indicated on the receipt before signing it. If so, then you should sign the receipt and fill in the date. It is very important that you accurately post the date, as it will likely mark the beginning of the 15 day rescission period.

THE CONTRACT. The contract (or purchase agreement) is the blueprint of the transaction. Every aspect of the deal between you and the developer must be in the contract.   Please review Chapter 7 of this book for considerations relating to the contract.

Name.   The first consideration in preparing the contract is your name.   When you identify yourself as purchaser in the first paragraph of the contract, your name should appear exactly the way you wish to take title. In other words, the name on the contract should be the same as the name that will be on the deed. If you are taking title with another person or persons, you should indicate in the contract whether such ownership will be as husband and wife, tenants in common, or joint tenants with a right of survivorship. A discussion of types of ownership is in Chapter 7 of this book.

Legal Description.   You should review the legal description in the contract to verify that the unit number contained in the contract corresponds to the unit you agreed to purchase.

Expenses. Customarily in a real estate transaction the seller pays the documentary stamp tax on the deed. However, in the sale of a new condominium unit, many developers structure the contract to require the purchaser to pay all closing expenses. This may be accomplished by a provision requiring the purchaser to pay the expenses outright at closing. Or in many cases, the contract calls for the developer to pay the documentary stamp tax and title insurance fee. In this situation, a "closing fee" is charged to the purchaser to reimburse the developer for these expenses. In either case, it is important for you to know what your expenses at closing will be.

Purchase Price and Deposit. The contract will set forth the purchase price of the unit. You should make sure that the price listed is the same as the price you agreed to. Also, confirm that all upgrade charges or costs for "extras" are included in the contract price. You don't want any surprises at closing.

You will also be required to pay a deposit at the time you sign the contract and possibly an additional deposit at a later date. The deposit is meant to show your good faith intention to purchase the unit. It also will be forfeited as liquidated damages if you default in the performance of the terms of the contract. Many purchasers who decide not to go through with the purchase will "walk away" from their deposit in exchange for cancellation of the contract. It is important that you realize that many contracts (in the default or remedies section) require forfeitures of not only the initial deposit but any later deposits, whether they have been paid or not.

If you complete the purchase, the deposits will be applied towards the purchase price at closing.

One of the differences in purchasing a condominium unit as opposed to a single family home is the treatment of the deposit. The Florida Condominium law requires that deposits up to ten percent of the purchase price must be held in escrow until the closing. But any deposit amounts in excess of ten percent of the purchase price may be used by the developer to pay actual construction expenses - *if authorized in the contract*. The law requires this authorization to be specified in bold print on the first page of the contract. This is important because if the developer defaults on the contract or does not complete your unit, the amount used for construction will be extremely difficult to recover.

After 2007, there were a number of developers who had purchasers cancel their contracts because of the downturn in the real estate market. Some of these developers had used a portion of the deposit to fund the construction. When they were unable to complete the project, the purchasers who did not forfeit their deposits were only able to recover the ten percent of the deposit not used for construction. They had to sue for the remaining amount. Many of these developers filed for bankruptcy and purchasers have yet to recover their full deposits.

Closing Date and Time for Completion of Construction. An extremely important provision of the contract is the closing date. If the unit you wish to purchase has been completed, a specific date may be set. You should make sure that this date allows you to arrange financing, if necessary, and is a date that is otherwise convenient to you.

In many new developments, the project has not been completed at the time many of the sales have been made. In these cases, the closing date is set as a date so many days after completion of construction, usually evidenced by a certificate of occupancy. The contract is required by law to give an *estimated* date of completion, and usually will state that the completion of construction will be no later than a certain date, usually two years after the signing of the contract. If construction is not completed by such date, you may rescind the contract and receive a full refund of your deposit, plus accrued interest, if applicable.

It is important that this deadline be included in the contract. Otherwise, you may be trapped in a transaction for however long a court determines "reasonable." Further, long delays in completion of construction may be symptoms of other problems the developer is having: inability to obtain construction financing, poor sales, problems with the quality of construction or other internal problems of the developer.

Keep in mind that it may be a long time after signing the contract before you can close and occupy your unit. A lot of things can change during that time. The real estate market could boom...or bust. The value of your unit at closing could greatly exceed the purchase price (good). Your financial and personal situation may change. All of these things will be factors in the availability and cost of your financing. There are many examples in Florida of units that went under contract in 2005, at the peak of the real estate boom, whose appraised value at the time of closing in 2007 had dropped to a fraction of the purchase price set forth on the contract.

Default and Remedy Provisions. If the developer can't deliver on his contractual promises, what happens then? Most contracts provide that you would be entitled to a full refund of your deposit (with interest, if applicable) and the right to pursue claims for specific performance or damages. Specific performance is the order of the court directing the developer to sell the unit to you. It is difficult to get and you probably should pursue this remedy only when the developer refuses to close because the value of the unit has increased and he believes he can get a higher price from a new buyer.

You want to make sure that, in the event you default in the performance of the contract, the developer's remedy is limited only to retaining your deposits under the contract as liquidated damages. Some contracts give the developer the right to "all deposits paid and agreed to be paid." In this case, if there is an additional deposit due, and you default prior to paying such additional deposit, the developer may be able to obtain a judgment for the amount of the second deposit as well as the one you already paid.

OTHER DOCUMENTS OF THE OFFERING.
As part of the seller's disclosure, the Florida Condominium Act requires that a buyer be provided with the condominium documents. These documents provide the

information that you will use to determine whether you wish to purchase a unit. The following is a brief description of each of the condominium documents.

DECLARATION OF CONDOMINIUM. Next to the contract, the Declaration of Condominium is the most important of the condominium documents.

- It is the document that creates the condominium.
- It provides a legal description of the land that will comprise the project,
- It specifies whether the development is a "phase condominium,"
- It describes any restrictions on the use, sale and lease of your unit and
- It sets forth your rights and responsibilities as an owner, among other things.

Generally, the first section of the declaration describes the land that will be submitted to the condominium form of ownership. When the declaration is recorded in the public records, the condominium is created. The developer must attach, as an exhibit, a survey and plot plan of the condominium showing where the units, amenities and other common areas are located.

Phase Condominiums. The developer has the option of creating the entire condominium project at once or in phases. If the developer decides to create a "phase condominium," it must tell you this in the declaration. The declaration must specify the number of phases, the number of units in each phase and a legal description and plot plan of each phase. Even though the declaration states that the developer intends to submit the future phases, the developer is under no obligation to do so. As a purchaser, you should check the declaration to see if the developer intends to build in phases. This is important because units and amenities described in phases other than the one your unit is in may never be built. This would mean that your share of the common expenses may be proportionally greater than if all of the proposed units were constructed. Also, the swimming pool or tennis court you were looking forward to may never be completed.

When reviewing the declaration, determine whether you will be buying into a phase condominium and, if so, whether it would be acceptable if your phase was the only one completed.

Share of Common Expenses. All of the expenses for the operation, maintenance and repair of the condominium property and the condominium association are divided among the unit owners. The condominium law provides that the units may share equally in these expenses or the allocation may be based upon the square footage of the unit in relation to the total square footage of all units in the condominium. The declaration of condominium will tell you which method the developer has chosen to divide these expenses. You should determine your share of the expenses keeping in mind that in a phase condominium all of the units may not be built.

Maintenance

The declaration describes which expenses for maintenance, alteration and repair the association is responsible for and which must be paid by you as a unit owner. Generally, all maintenance and repairs to the common elements are borne by the association and the unit owner is responsible for those within the boundaries of the unit. You should review this provision to determine who is responsible for incidental damage to a unit caused by the association during repair of a common element. For example, if a wall has to be damaged to determine the source of a leak which the association is responsible for, will the association be responsible for the repair of the unit wall? If so, will this include replacement of paint or wallpaper?

Insurance

The association is responsible for acquiring and maintaining casualty and flood (if applicable) insurance to cover the common elements and the apartment buildings. The cost of the premium is a common expense that is included in your maintenance fee. This insurance specifically does not cover the interior of a unit (floor coverings, wall coverings, electrical fixtures, appliances, cabinets and furniture). You are responsible for acquiring insurance for your contents and interior.

The declaration specifies the manner in which any insurance proceeds will be applied, and usually provides that, if it is determined the buildings and improvements will not be reconstructed or repaired, then the proceeds will be divided among the unit owners.

Limited Common Elements. Many condominium projects have areas that are not part of a unit but are used only by a particular unit owner. The areas are known as limited common elements. Examples of limited common elements are parking spaces, garages, storage areas and boat docks. They are assigned to a specific unit and may or may not be transferable with the unit. The declaration tells you how you can transfer your limited common elements and whether you or the association is responsible for maintenance and repairs of the limited common elements.

Many times a purchase of a unit will include exclusive use of a separate parking space. In such a case, you should determine what rights you have in the parking space including whether you can transfer it to another unit owner without transferring your unit.

Assessment Liens. Florida law and the declaration give the association authority to create a budget for the association expenses. It then divides the amounts necessary to cover these expenses among the unit owners in the form of maintenance assessments. The assessment is payable either monthly or quarterly. Your payment of the assessment is secured by a lien against your unit and, if it is not paid, the association has the right to foreclose the unit.

Restrictions of Resale and Leasing. An important consideration when reviewing the declaration is the association's right to restrict the resale and leasing of your unit. Many declarations provide the association with the right to approve the sale or lease of a unit. In many condominiums, if you wished to sell or lease your unit, you would have to present the signed contract or lease to the board of directors. They may also require background information on the prospective purchaser. The board of directors would then have a certain time period to review this information and either approve or disapprove of the sale.

Another is to provide the association with a right of first refusal. Under this procedure the unit owner/seller is required to provide the contract to sell his or her unit to the association. The association then has the right to purchase the unit at the same price and on the same terms and conditions as the original contract. If the association does not purchase the unit within a specified time, you are free to sell to your original purchaser.

It is important that you review these provisions with your intended use of the unit in mind. If you are purchasing the unit as an investment with the intent to lease it to generate income, you should make sure that the restrictions against leasing, if any, do not make purchasing the unit impractical as an investment. If you are purchasing the unit to be your home, you probably want to make sure that the declaration doesn't allow transient rentals.

Read these provisions carefully. The leasing policy usually has more impact on determining the atmosphere and character of the community than any other factor.

Use Restrictions. This is the section that tells you things such as how many persons can occupy the unit, whether you may keep a pet in the unit and, if so, what kind and how large. This is another section that you should read carefully as each condominium project is different in this regard. You should be comfortable that you will be allowed to do the things you wish. You should also look at it from the viewpoint of what your neighbor will be permitted to do. Keep in mind that, in many cases, there is only a wall separating you from your neighbor, so the use restrictions can become very important.

Plot Plans and Floor Plans. Every Declaration of Condominium has, as an exhibit to it, a survey of the property upon which the condominium project is built, which specifies the exact location of each unit, the common elements and the limited common elements. The exhibit will also contain floor plans of each type of unit in the project, which show the location and dimensions of each room.

You should cross check the plot plan with the unit number on your purchase contract to make sure you are purchasing the unit you bargained for. You can also check the location of limited common elements such as parking or boat docks.

Also, review the floor plans to confirm that the size and layout of the unit is the same as what was presented to you during the sales process.

ESTIMATED OPERATING BUDGET. The estimated operating budget discloses the developer's calculations of the annual expenses it believes will be needed to operate the association and maintain the common elements.

The document provides the estimated expenses for certain categories such as management fees, pest control, insurance, common area utilities and repairs. It divides the total expenses by the number of units to determine each unit's assessment.

The condominium law also requires each association to set aside reserve funds for anticipated future repair and replacement of major items such as roof replacement, parking area resurfacing, building, painting and repairs. These funds allow the cost for the major items to be collected gradually instead of being financed by a large special assessment against the unit owners when the roof needs to be replaced.

When purchasing a condominium unit from a prior owner it is important to review the reserve accounts. Underfunded reserve accounts in an older project usually result in large special assessments to the unit owners in the future.

Developer Guarantee. Once a unit is submitted to condominium by filing the Declaration of Condominium, its owner is liable for payments of assessments. The developer is the owner of all unsold units and is liable for payment of the full monthly assessment on every one of them. Because this can be a large expense to a developer that has just built and financed the project, the condominium law provides some relief to the developer.

First, the developer has the option to build the condominium project in phases. This gives the developer the right to develop the project over a period of time, submitting units to the condominium in phases, without obligating the developer to construct all of the phases. The developer is only liable for assessments on units in phases actually submitted to the condominium.

The second form of relief to the developer is the developer guarantee. Under this program, the developer sets an assessment amount that the new buyers will have to pay each month and guarantees that the amount will not increase for a certain period of time. If these set assessments paid by the buyers are not sufficient to cover all of the common expenses, the developer must pay the shortfall. In exchange for this guarantee, the developer is excused from paying assessments against the unsold units during that time period.

The guarantee must be stated in either the purchase contract, the declaration, the offering prospectus or a written agreement between the developer and a majority of the unit owners.

What this means is that the developer will provide a monthly or quarterly assessment in the condominium documents. If the actual expenses exceed the budgeted amount or if there are not enough purchased units so that the assessments collected are not sufficient to pay the expenses, the developer will pay the shortfall.

The developer guarantee can be beneficial to you because it allows the developer to keep the assessments low during the guarantee period. You may, however, experience a sharp increase in assessments after the guarantee period expires.

PURCHASE DEPOSIT ESCROW AGREEMENT. The Purchase Deposit Escrow Agreement is an agreement between the developer and the escrow agent which governs the manner in which your deposit will be held.

FREQUENTLY ASKED QUESTION AND ANSWER SHEET. The developer must furnish a one page document of questions and answers that purchasers most often ask when buying a unit. Most of the answers refer you to the document (Declaration of Condominium, Estimated Operating Budget, etc.) where the information can be found.

RECEIPT FOR CONDOMINIUM DOCUMENTS. At the time you enter into a contract to purchase a unit, the developer must provide the above-described documents to you and obtain a receipt from you for those documents. The receipt must itemize the documents that were delivered to you.

It is important that you review the receipt to ensure that you have received all the documents that it indicates. Your signature on the receipt is the evidence that the developer will use if it needs to prove that the documents were properly delivered.

Also, make sure that you accurately state the date on the receipt as it could be used to begin the 15 day right of recession on the contract.

TRANSITION FROM DEVELOPER CONTROL

During the development and construction period of the project, the developer has control of the condominium association. It elects the board of directors and officers and has full authority to create the budget and determine assessments.

There is a point where the developer is required to begin turning over control of the association to the purchaser unit owners. This transition, commonly called the "turnover," begins after 15% of the total number of units has been sold.

While most of the intricacies of turnover are beyond the scope of this book, there are some important aspects that may affect your decision to buy.

At the completion of the turnover, the developer is required to have the financial records of the association, from incorporation of the association through the date of turnover audited by an independent certified public accountant.

If you are purchasing a unit within a year after the turnover date, you should request a copy of the audit from the association. You should also have the association provide in writing a certification that the association is not involved in any litigation, including litigation against the developer and that no litigation is pending. If there is litigation, the unit owners will be responsible for paying the association's attorneys' fees and they could be considerable.

You should also review the latest financial statements of the association and the reserve fund balances. You want to make sure the association is not in financial distress, as this will almost certainly lead to large special assessments against the unit owners.

Speaking of special assessments, you should ask the association whether any have been assessed, authorized or proposed. In most contracts the seller is responsible for special assessments that have already been assessed and the buyer will be stuck with any that are authorized and assessed after closing. It is important to ask other unit owners to find out if any special assessment is imminent.

Remember, if you are purchasing from a unit owner other than the developer, your right to cancel after signing the contract is only 3 days. All of your investigations and due diligence must be done within that time.

CHAPTER 9

Building Your Home In Florida

There are many advantages to having your home built instead of buying a new one. Everything is brand new. The thoughts of repairs and their expenses and inconvenience are far off in the future. You can choose the design and features you want. You determine the quality of construction. This can truly be your dream home.

Choosing the Right Builder. There are challenges to having your home built. The first and arguably the most important is choosing the right builder.

A large number of factors must be considered when choosing a builder. First and foremost, you must choose a builder that fits into your budget.

There are two general categories of builders to choose from: spec home builders and custom builders. The line between the two has been blurred as some spec home builders will add custom features to their construction.

Spec home builders usually offer the lowest prices. They have a portfolio of standard designs or model homes which they construct in volume. As a result they have the construction process down to an efficient system. Each type of model home is built the same every time allowing for savings in costs.

Aside from the cost, there are other advantages to selecting a spec home builder. You can see a completed model home to evaluate the design and the quality of work. Since the builder has a system for constructing the model home, the construction period is usually shorter. The builder usually has a standard menu for choosing floor coverings, color schemes, cabinets and countertops. This makes the selection process easier and the cost is generally set. Many builders construct multiple homes in a subdivision which allows them to easily schedule subcontractors and material delivery. This makes the construction process faster and results in significant savings.

The drawback of choosing a spec home builder is that any change in the plans which results in re-engineering such as moving load bearing walls may not be allowed by the builder. If it is allowed, it will usually result in a sharp increase in cost and significant delay in the completion.

Custom builders start with a blank slate and design the home from scratch. With a custom builder, you can have a unique, one-of-a-kind design and include your selection of features.

Obviously, the creation of unique plans and incorporations of custom materials and features will require more money out of your pocket.

Hurricane Protection. Moving to Florida brings with it new and different issues than those you faced back home. One of these issues that you must consider in the construction of your home is hurricane protection.

In 1992, Hurricane Andrew devastated the Homestead area of Dade County. This led to extensive building code reform throughout the state. If you took the time to review each county's building code, you would find that the level of hurricane protection required varies from county to county. While Dade County has high protection standards that a few other counties have adopted, many of the other counties require only that homes are built to withstand Category 2 storms.

Consider that Katrina in 2005 was a Category 4 hurricane when it made landfall and that several Category 2 or higher storms hit Florida in 2004 alone.

As a result, some builders offer construction that exceeds their county's requirements. You should strongly consider finding a builder whose homes are designed and built to withstand Category 4 storms. The cost of this added protection will be high, however, it could be money well spent. Also, you will be eligible for discounts on your homeowners insurance premium as you will see in the next Chapter.

Making the Decision. You should make a budget to see the price you can afford for your new home. You can then decide between a spec home or custom home and select your level of hurricane protection. This will narrow your choice of builders.

Next, you should make a list of the builders in the area who meet the above criteria. If you will use a spec home builder, it should have lots available in the area where you want to build.

Most builders have published information or a website outlining their experience and describing the work they do. When you find builders that impress you, you should personally visit their offices. You will form a valuable impression from this meeting. Was the builder's representative courteous, professional? Did they adequately answer your questions and provide complete information? Do they have a model or floor plans that you like? What selections and options do they offer? Do they offer financing? A home warranty? You should ask these and other questions and pay close attention not only to the answers, but also the manner in which the answers are given. Is the builder's representative forthright or does he give vague and elusive answers.

Don't make your decision solely on your meeting with a salesperson. Insist on speaking with the owner or a construction manager. If you choose this builder, you will be working with them for a period of months, so it is important that you feel comfortable with them.

Finally, inquire around town about the builder's reputation. Demand references from the builder and contact them. Talk to real estate professionals, attorneys and insurance agents in the area.

Remember, this will be a considerable investment of your time and money. Make sure you do your homework completely.

THE CONSTRUCTION CONTRACT. The issues surrounding the drafting of the construction contract are too numerous and intricate to completely cover in this book. What this section will do is address a few of the major issues involved in negotiating and drafting a residential construction contract. This is an area where it is imperative that you hire an attorney to represent your interests.

Every construction contract must be in writing. There are too many provisions that need to be addressed, too many details and too many time constraints to rely on a verbal agreement.

Usually the builder or general contractor will have its standard form of contract. These must be reviewed carefully to make sure that your interests and rights are protected. The following is a list of some of the issues addressed or that need to be addressed by the contract.

What is Being Built? The contract should incorporate as an exhibit the building plans and specifications showing exactly what construction is to be accomplished. There should also be a paragraph which specifies whether a builder may substitute materials and fixtures. If allowed, the provision should require that any substituted materials be of the same or greater quality than the original.

Who Is Building It? The contract must name the contractor that is responsible for building the house. It should provide the name of a contact person and an address where correspondence is to be sent.

The contract will only name the general contractor as a party. Because you have a direct written contract with the contractor, it is deemed to be "in privity" with you. This distinction is important with respect to the Florida Construction Lien Law and will be addressed later in this Chapter. The subcontractors and material suppliers are not parties to this contract. They usually enter into a contract with the general contractor who is responsible for overseeing their work and paying them.

Where Is It Being Built? The contract should contain the legal description of the property on which the house is being built.

How Much Will It Cost To Build It? The purchase price or construction price is one of the most important issues to both sides of the contract. The builder usually has a set price to construct a specific model home. It may adjust that price based on a number of factors including lot condition and materials cost. Those adjustments should be made prior to entering into the construction contract.

You, as the person paying, want as much certainty in the price as possible. The contractor doesn't want to fully bear the risk of escalating costs and would like the purchase price to be flexible.

It is important to consider that the builder orders and negotiates the price for most of the materials at the start of the job. This greatly reduces the risk to the builder that it will have to pay increased costs for materials.

If the home is one of the builder's models, the price charged by the subcontractors is set. If your home is a custom design, the builder has obtained bids from subcontractors and material suppliers prior to the start of construction. In any case, the purchase price of your construction contract should be firm.

Another concern of the builder is that construction may not begin in a timely manner after the construction contract is signed. This would increase its risk of having to pay higher than anticipated costs for labor and materials. To address this, many contracts include a clause stating that prices quoted in the construction contract are binding on the builder only if construction is started within 60 days. If permits cannot be obtained or if the buyer is unable to arrange financing within this time, the builder would have the right to cancel the contract and the parties would have to renegotiate the purchase price.

Change Orders. In many cases it may become necessary to change aspects of the building plans to meet the owner's wishes or to comply with local building ordinances. This request to change the building plans, whether made by the owner or the contractor, is called a change order. The construction contract should require that all change orders be in writing and signed by both the contractor and the owner.

The written change order should describe the change, contain any adjustment to the construction price and specify any resulting change in the time of completion. The contract should state that no changes in the plans or the construction price are to be made unless specified by a change order.

Change orders become a part of the construction contract and are treated as an amendment to the contract. If there is an increase in the construction price required by the change order, the owner will usually have to pay it at the time the change order is signed.

Allowances. Many times the owner will have choices as to the type and quality of items such as appliances, carpeting and fixtures. Typically, the purchase price contains allowances for those items. If an item you select results in costs that exceed the allowance for that item, the difference will be added to the purchase price. In most cases this does not require a change order.

For example, if the construction contract states that a standard dishwasher in the contractor's model package costs $500, and you decide to upgrade to a dishwasher costing $800, you will receive an allowance for $500 toward the upgraded dishwasher and $300 will be added to the construction price.

When Will It Be Built And How Long Will It Take? The construction contract should always contain a commencement date and a completion date. Most of the time these dates are not defined as specific calendar days.

The construction contract usually calls for the commencement date to be no longer than so many days after signing the contract or, if a mortgage is involved, so many days after the mortgage closing.

What constitutes the start of construction should also be specified. Some examples used in construction contracts are the date on which the house footings are poured or, if there are no footings, the day on which the installation of rough plumbing is begun.

The completion date is usually set as the date that the construction is "substantially complete." It is commonly required to be a set number of days after the start of construction. It is important to understand the term, "substantially complete' in the context of construction contracts. "Substantially complete" is generally defined as the date on which the Certificate of Occupancy is issued. In most cases there are still some punchlist items that must be completed, such as paint touch-up at the time the Certificate of Occupancy is issued. This does not prevent the house from being substantially complete.

Insurance. Most construction contracts place requirements for obtaining and maintaining insurance on both the contractor and the owner.

If you are the owner of the building lot and a worker is injured during construction, you can bet you will be named in a lawsuit. For this reason, you should make sure that the contractor carries worker's compensation insurance. This covers any damages arising from injuries to persons working under the contractor. The contract should also require all subcontractors hired by the general contractor to carry worker's compensation.

You should also make sure that Builder's Risk insurance is required under the contract. The purpose of Builder's Risk insurance is to insure against loss to the project during construction. It covers losses such as loss of use, repair and reconstruction costs. This coverage can be paid to the owner, the contractor or both.

All insurance required by the construction contract must be obtained through an insurance company authorized to do business in the State of Florida. You should obtain copies of certificates of insurance for these policies.

"Occurrence" vs. "Claims Made" Policy. When obtaining insurance you often have the option between "occurrence" or "claims made" coverage. "Occurrence" policies provide coverage for claims only if they occurred during the coverage period of the policy <u>and</u> the claims are made during that period.

A "claims made" policy covers claims occurring during the coverage period even if the claim is not made during such period.

If it all possible, you should attempt to obtain "claims made" coverage as it provides coverage for a much greater length of time.

How Does The Builder Get Paid? It is typical for the contractor to receive partial payments of the construction price throughout the construction of the home. These payments are usually triggered by the completion of a certain aspect of the construction. For example, the contract may provide that the contractor will receive payment equal to 10% of the construction price when the framing of the house is completed.

These payments and the times they are payable should be specified in the contract. This is done in the "draw schedule."

The draw schedule should always provide that a partial payment or "draw" is made only upon completion of specified work. If you are financing the construction using a bank, the bank will arrange for a qualified person to inspect the property to make sure the required work has been completed. Only then will the bank release the draw.

If you are not financing the construction, you should arrange for your own inspections. Contact a local bank to find the names of qualified inspectors. Some banks and escrow companies also provide a service under which they will hold the construction funds, arrange for the inspections and disburse the draws according to the terms of the contract. The cost of this service is usually money well spent. Especially if you are living in another state.

The contract should make the payment of a draw contingent upon certain conditions. Before the contractor is paid, the following should have occurred:

1. Certification is obtained from a qualified inspector that the work required to receive the draw has been completed in a satisfactory manner.

2. Releases of Lien are obtained from all subcontractors and suppliers who have provided services or materials. The importance of the Release of Lien will be discussed in the section about the Florida Construction Lien law.

Before the final payment is made, you should obtain from the general contractor a contractor's affidavit as required by the Florida Construction Lien law. In this document the contractor certifies under oath that all labor and materials going into the job have been paid for in full and that there is no construction lien which can be filed against the property after completion of the job. If funds from the final draw are to be used to pay for part of the labor and materials going into the job, those items unpaid at the time the affidavit is to be furnished must be listed in the affidavit and you have the right to make payments directly to those subcontractors and suppliers listed.

What Other Costs Are There? Counties and municipalities impose impact fees on new construction to help pay for the additional services required as a result of your new house. You should find out from the county or city what impact fees will be assessed and prepare to pay those.

Other miscellaneous expenses are usually incurred in construction of a home. Items such as installation of utility meters, water and sewer hookup fees, and, if applicable, the cost of engineering and installing a septic system or groundwater well may be needed.

These costs are customarily borne by the owner. Some may be listed in the contract as allowances.

Warranties. Under common law the owner is given implied warranties of habitability, merchantability and fitness for a particular purpose. This means that the contractor is deemed to warrant that the house is built in such a manner as to be able to be occupied by the owners.

Many construction contracts will exclude these common law warranties in favor of an express warranty described in the contract. Review this warranty carefully.

What If There Are Problems? Most contracts are vague about what constitutes a default by the contractor and even more vague about how to resolve it.

This makes it extremely important for you, or an inspector hired by you, to continuously inspect the progress of the work. If there is a problem with following the plans or with the workmanship, you need to be aware of it as early as possible. This reduces the time and expense of making corrections.

You should add the following provision to the contract to protect your interests:

> "The contractor shall correct any work that fails to conform to the requirements of the contract and the plans and specifications where such failure to conform appears during the progress of the construction, and shall remedy any defects due to faulty materials or workmanship which appear during the warranty period."

If there are serious defects or if the contractor fails to abide by the terms of the contract, you are usually given the right to notify the contractor of the problem and, if he fails to correct it, either have the corrections made yourself and deduct the cost from the construction price or terminate the contract.

Again, this shows the need for staying on top of the work and addressing these issued as they arise. Construction litigation is a nasty, time consuming and very expensive process. Every day there are cases that delay an owner from completing and moving into his new home for months and even years.

The chance of running into these problems is greatly reduced by choosing the right builder and monitoring the progress of the construction.

THE FLORIDA CONSTRUCTION LIEN LAW. This is an issue that can cause more financial damage to the unwary than any other aspect of the construction process. Every contractor, subcontractor and supplier who provides materials or services for the construction of your home has a right to be paid. If any of them is not paid in full, that person or company has a right to enforce their claim for payment by filing a construction lien.

This seems simple on the surface. A contractor or subcontractor works on the construction and you pay him for his work. However, the simplicity ends when you consider that you have a contract only with the general contractor to build your house. The general contractor then hires subcontractors to perform such services as installing the electrical system, plumbing and roofing. The general contractor usually negotiates a price with the subcontractor which is paid from funds the general contractor receives from you.

The problems arise when you pay the general contractor for work that was done but the general contractor does not pay the subcontractor who actually did the work. Unable to obtain payment for the work from the general contractor, the subcontractor will look to you, the owner, for payment. You tell the subcontractor that you have already paid for that work and, additionally, you only have a contract with the general contractor, not him. You advise him to go back to the general contractor to get his payment.

A few days later you receive a letter in the mail notifying you that the subcontractor has filed a construction lien against your property in an attempt to enforce his claim for payment. Within the next few weeks you receive more letters informing you of more liens. By the time you add them all up, you're shocked to discover there are subcontractors and suppliers claiming payments of tens of thousands of dollars are owed to them.

You quickly hire a lawyer to straighten this whole mess out. After reviewing all of the paperwork, your lawyer informs you that the liens are valid and if you do not pay the subcontractors, they have the right to foreclose on your property and have it sold at public auction to pay their claims.

In a panic, you ask your lawyer to contact the general contractor and do whatever it takes to force him to pay the subcontractors with the money you have already paid. Your lawyer sadly informs you that the general contractor has shut down his business leaving about a dozen other customers in the same position as you: an unfinished house riddled with claims of liens. Rumor has it that he's now living in Costa Rica.

How can you avoid a similar disaster? The next part of this chapter explains how the Florida Construction Lien Law works and shows you how to keep from getting caught in the dilemma you just read.

Who can file a lien? Basically, anyone who performs work or provides materials for the construction of your home can file a lien. There is an important distinction between those with whom you have a direct contract and those who have a subcontract with another contractor.

In most cases you will only have a direct contract with the general contractor. The general contractor will contract with subcontractors such as electricians, plumbers and suppliers to help build the house. The general contractor will be responsible to pay these subcontractors out of the contract price he receives from you. You will have no direct contract with the subcontractors. In fact, many owners never know who the subcontractors are.

A contractor who has a direct contract with you can claim a lien against your property by recording a claim of lien form in the public records of the county where the home is located. He can file the claim of lien any time during the progress of the work or any time up to 90 days after furnishing the final work or materials.

The law is very detailed and specific about what contractors and subcontractors must do to acquire a valid lien. If they do not follow the law to the letter, they will almost always lose their right to the lien.

Any person or company who does not have a direct contract with you, but instead has contracted with the general contractor or another subcontractor, is defined not to be in privity with you. A subcontractor or supplier who is not in privity with the owner must jump through an additional hoop to obtain a valid lien.

Not only must he timely file a claim of lien, he must first serve a "Notice to Owner" on you. The Notice to Owner informs you that this subcontractor is working on the construction of your home. It is usually sent to you by certified mail. It cannot be sent more than 45 days after he begins work or supplies materials.

The Notice to Owner is very ominous looking. It contains a "WARNING TO OWNER" at the top of the form in all capital letters. Many owners panic when they receive it, thinking that a lien has been filed against their property. Don't be alarmed when you receive it. It is simply a notification of who is working on your home.

You should keep all Notice to Owner forms that you receive *and* the envelope in which they arrived. I will discuss the importance of this step later.

Notice Of Commencement. Before construction begins, you as the owner, will be required to record a Notice of Commencement in the public records of the county in which the property is located. The Notice of Commencement identifies you as the owner of the property, the lender financing the construction (if any) and addresses of all persons who will receive notices regarding the construction (such as Notices to Owner and Claims of Lien). In addition to recording the Notice of Commencement, a copy of it must be posted at the construction site.

The general contractor or lender will usually provide the Notice of Commencement form. Review it carefully and make sure the names and addresses are correct.

If you are taking out a loan to finance the construction, the lender will require that the mortgage be recorded prior to the Notice of Commencement. If you or the contractor jump the gun and record the Notice of Commencement first, the lender will require that it be terminated and a new Notice of Commencement be recorded. This is a time consuming process so you should consult with your attorney or the lender before recording the Notice of Commencement.

How To Protect Yourself

There are some basic procedures you should follow to protect yourself from construction liens.

1. File or make sure someone files the Notice of Commencement before construction begins.

2. Obtain from the general contractor a copy of the construction budget with a summary of the subcontractor bids.

3. Obtain from the general contractor a list of all subcontractors and suppliers who have a subcontract (with the general contractor and not you) to provide services or materials to your property.

4. Keep all Notices to Owner that you receive from the subcontractors and suppliers together with the envelope in which they came. You might remember that the subcontractor has 45 days from the time he started his work to send you the Notice to Owner or he will lose his right to file a lien. The envelope contains a postmark that is evidence of whether or not he met that requirement.

5. Before making any partial payment, obtain a Partial Release of Lien from each subcontractor and supplier who has worked on or supplied materials to your property to that date.

   The Partial Release of Lien is a written statement that says that the subcontractor or supplier has been paid in full by the general contractor up to a certain date. By signing it, the subcontractor waives its right to file a lien for non-payment for any work or materials provided prior to the date specified on the statement.

6. Before making the final payment to the general contractor, you should obtain a contractor's affidavit. The Contractor's Affidavit is a written statement made by the general contractor under oath that states either, (1) all subcontractors and suppliers have been paid in full, or, (2) if all subcontractors and suppliers have not been paid in full, the amount due to each.

   Florida law requires that the general contractor present the owner with the Contractor's Affidavit or he has no lien or right of action (right to file a lawsuit) against the owner.

   The general contractor should also obtain releases of liens from all of the subcontractors and suppliers to back up the Contractor's Affidavit and provide them to you.

7. Prepare a list of all "punch list" items for the contractor to complete and have the general contractor agree in writing to complete these items within a certain time period.

8. Before making any partial or final payment, the construction should be inspected on your behalf by an engineer, architect or other professional to make sure that the work called for in the draw schedule has been completed.

   If you are financing the construction, the lender will usually arrange for the inspection before releasing any funds. The lender also will obtain the Partial Release of Lien. If this is the case, make sure you get a copy of all of these documents at the time the lender receives them.

Also, if you are financing the construction, provide the lender with a copy of all Notices to Owner you receive and the Contractor's Affidavit.

9. Make sure the general contractor provides you with copies of all building permits and insurance documents.

CHAPTER 10

Insuring Your Florida Home

Property insurance has been one of the most heated issues facing Floridians in the last few years. There are a number of factors that create a challenge for insurers and homeowners alike.

- Property values in Florida have increased dramatically resulting in an increase in premiums.
- The cost of construction, including building materials and labor, has also risen dramatically.
- More people are choosing to live on the coast which has increased risk.
- Florida is susceptible to tropical storms and hurricanes.
- Older homes do not meet the new building codes which provide increased protection from wind.

In order to obtain coverage from a quality insurer at a reasonable cost, it is important that you have as much information as possible.

If you finance your home through a mortgage, the lender will require that you obtain homeowners insurance and maintain it during the life of the loan. When your mortgage is paid off, insurance is no longer required; however, I recommend that you continue to maintain it.

Many lenders require their borrowers to pay their insurance premiums into an escrow account each month as a part of their loan payment. When the premium comes due, the lender pays the insurer out of the escrow account.

Even though the lender pays the premium, you are responsible for choosing the insurance company and acquiring the policy.

Types of Coverage. Your homeowners insurance policy will generally consist of two types of coverage: casualty and liability.

Casualty insurance protects you from damage to your home from manmade and natural causes such as fire, lightning, hail and theft.

Liability insurance covers you for accidents that occur on your property for which you are held responsible.

An important type of coverage that is not included in your homeowners policy is flood insurance. Because of the proximity to water of almost all property in Florida, you should strongly consider flood insurance.

If you have a mortgage and live in a flood hazard zone, your lender will require flood insurance. If you don't have a mortgage, flood insurance is optional.

Flood insurance covers damage from water caused by natural flooding and by leaking pipes in your home. Also, damage from storm surge during a hurricane will only be covered by flood insurance. This became a major issue after Hurricane Katrina in 2005, when many Mississippi residents tried to obtain coverage from their homeowners policies for damage caused by the storm surge. It was finally determined that even if the waves were caused by the wind, homeowners policies would not cover the flood damage.

You can obtain the flood policy from the agent writing your homeowners policy; however, flood insurance is underwritten by the National Flood Insurance Program.

WHAT YOU NEED TO LOOK FOR WHEN BUYING INSURANCE. Premiums for homeowners insurance in Florida have been increasing. Many homeowners have tried to lower their premiums by reducing their coverage. This isn't always your best alternative. You should become familiar with all of the components of your insurance coverage. This will come up with the most efficient and cost effective way to protect your home.

Choosing Your Policy Limits. Your home should be insured for at least 80 percent of its value. This is based on the value of the structure and improvements, excluding the land. Many lenders will require a minimum amount of coverage, usually based on the purchase price or the mortgage amount. This is usually not enough to cover the cost of rebuilding your home.

The idea is to make sure the insurance proceeds are adequate to replace your home if it is destroyed. You also need to consider what that cost will be in the future. This is where a good insurance agent can be a tremendous benefit. Aside from explaining the complexity of the policy and its coverage, she can advise you on increases in local building costs and changes to the building code that may make replacement more expensive.

Some insurance policies give you the option of an inflation rider. This will automatically adjust the coverage to take into account increased construction costs in your area.

In order to make sure you get proper coverage, you should have an estimate made of the replacement value of your home. There are a couple of web sites that help you do this such as www.accucoverage.com and www.insuretovalue.net. If your home has unusual or expensive features, you can always have a professional appraisal done.

Most homeowners insurance policies also provide coverage for personal property such as furniture, appliances, clothing, jewelry, and other contents of your home. The coverage is usually set at a certain percentage of your coverage on the structure. When reviewing the policy, look at Section 1, Coverage C, Contents, on the Declarations page to see what the limits are. If you have expensive jewelry or electronics, you may want to increase the limits.

Do You Have Replacement Cost Coverage? A policy with replacement cost coverage pays for the replacement of damaged property. If your roof is blown off in a storm, replacement cost coverage will pay for installation of a new roof. Without replacement cost coverage, the policy will deduct depreciation for wear and tear based on the age of your roof. You would be required to pay the remaining cost to replace it.

Most policies provide replacement cost coverage, and flood insurance for the structure is usually available at replacement cost. Even if you have replacement cost, the coverage may be capped at the policy limits.

You may also be able to purchase an option called extended replacement cost coverage. If you've been there after a major storm, you will have noticed that construction materials and labor were scarce. As a result, the cost to replace a home immediately increased.

In a situation like that, the cost to replace your home could increase beyond your policy limits. To protect yourself, you can purchase an extended replacement cost policy which will pay an additional 20 to 25 percent above the policy limits.

It is important that you adjust your coverage to meet increased construction costs, since failure to do so may cause your coverage to be insufficient, even with extended replacement cost coverage.

For your personal property items, you have the option of insuring for actual cash value or replacement cost. An actual cash value policy will pay you the cost of your property minus depreciation. The replacement cost policy pays you the amount needed to replace the items.

Usually the premium for a replacement cost policy is about 10 percent higher than the actual cash value policy. You can also obtain personal property coverage with your flood insurance policy. However, you can only get actual cash value coverage.

You should check your personal property coverage carefully because even if your policy insures for replacement cost on your home, it may not for your personal property.

Law and Ordinance Coverage. Imagine that you buy a beautiful older home in a prestigious neighborhood. Unfortunately, a fire severely damages it, destroying three-quarters of the house. When you undertake to rebuild the home, you discover the building code has significantly changed since the house was first built.

In order to obtain a building permit, your construction plans must show an increase in the elevation of the living area as well as many other upgrades to comply with the new building code.

Now your insurance company tells you that your homeowners policy won't pay the additional cost required to comply with the new code.

In order to prevent this lapse in coverage, you will need to purchase a "Law and Ordinance" endorsement to your policy. This will provide coverage up to a specified amount to pay additional costs required to meet new building codes.

Windstorm Coverage. One of the most expensive parts of your insurance coverage is windstorm coverage. This covers damage from wind events such as hurricanes or tornadoes. Its premiums can be up to half of the total policy premiums. After July 1, 2007, windstorm coverage became optional. However, almost all lenders require it. Although dropping windstorm coverage will save a lot of money on your premium, it is not recommended.

Screen Enclosures. Many Florida homes have swimming pools surrounded by a screen enclosure. Their owners often assume that the screen enclosure is covered along with the house structure. This in not always a good assumption.

Review your policy to see how screen enclosures are treated. Some insurance companies require optional additional coverage in order to replace a damaged screen enclosure. Other companies have a cap on the amount they will cover. Since some pool enclosures can run in the tens of thousands of dollars, it is important to know where you stand with your insurer.

Mold. If your home is damaged by water, Florida's humid climate is very conducive to mold growth on walls, ceilings, and carports. Just as with screen enclosures, insurance companies treat mold infestation differently.

Some policies don't cover the removal of mold while others require optional coverage. Make sure you know how, or even if, your policy treats removal of mold.

Temporary Living Expenses. If your home is damaged by fire or a storm to a point where it is uninhabitable, not only are you dealing with the cost of repair and replacement, but also the cost of temporarily living elsewhere while the repairs are made. Most homeowners policies provide coverage for these expenses. This loss of use coverage typically pays for hotels, meals, and other living expenses.

The coverage is usually limited to a specified amount sometimes based on a percentage of the coverage on your house. Some insurers allow you to purchase additional higher coverage.

You should be aware that flood insurance does not include this coverage for temporary living expenses. So if the damage to your home is solely from flooding or storm surge, you are on your own.

Deductibles. One way to reduce your cost of premiums is to increase your deductible. A deductible is the amount toward damages that you pay before the insurer begins to pay. By making the deductible amount higher, you are sharing the risk with the insurance company. For that reason, the insurer is willing to accept a lower premium.

The standard deductibles for homeowners policies are either $500 or $1,000 for claims other than those related to hurricanes. You should ask your insurance agent how much savings an increase in deductible would give you. Also, before raising your deductible, you need to make sure it does not violate the terms of your mortgage, if you have one.

If you increase your deductible to an amount greater than 5 or 10 percent of your insured value, it may be a good idea to create an emergency reserve account. This will ensure that you have cash in the event of a large claim.

Homeowners policies in Florida have a separate deductible for hurricanes. Your hurricane deductible is usually 2 percent of the insured value. You can save a considerable amount on premiums by increasing your hurricane deductible. You have to weigh this against the potential risk.

For example, if you have a 2 percent hurricane deductible and suffer $300,000 in damages from a hurricane, you would pay for the first $6,000 of those damages, not the $500 you may pay for non-hurricane damages. An increase to 5 percent hurricane deductible puts you on the hook for the first $15,000 in damages. Make sure you know your hurricane deductible.

You should also know that a non-hurricane deductible on your policy could apply to hurricanes. Under Florida law, your hurricane deductible is calculated per year, not per storm. If you suffer damage from a second storm in the same year and your hurricane deductible has already been met by the first storm, you will have to pay another deductible, known as the "all perils" deductible. It is usually the same as your non-hurricane deductible.

Tips to Reduce Your Premium. Many homeowners pay more for their insurance than they have to. By being alert and selecting only options and coverages that pertain to your situation, you can reduce your premium by omitting certain coverage and qualifying for discounts. This, together with raising your deductibles, can result in considerable savings.

Some ideas to consider are:

1. Take advantage of discounts for improvements to your home that protect it from storm damage. Securing your roof trusses, installing hurricane shutters, and strengthening your garage doors are just some of the improvements that can result in significant discounts. Your insurance agent can provide you with a list of these improvements and certified inspectors can rate your house or one that you are looking to buy.

2. As I mentioned earlier, most homeowners policies provide coverage for your personal property at a fixed percentage of the amount of insurance you have on the house. Many times this is well in excess of the actual value of your personal property. You are paying for insurance you don't need. Determine the actual replacement value of your personal property and adjust your coverage to meet it.

3. Make sure you have sufficient coverage for your homeowners policy. If you are looking to save money on premiums, raise the deductible, don't reduce your coverage.

Citizens Insurance. In 2002, the Florida Legislature created the Citizens Property Insurance Corporation to provide insurance to homeowners who cannot obtain coverage in the private insurance market.

After the storm saturated year of 2004, many property and casualty insurance companies pulled out of the Florida market. This made it difficult and sometimes impossible for some homeowners to acquire insurance.

Citizens was able to be the insurer of last resort for those homeowners. By law, Citizens writes policies only for homeowners who cannot find insurance on the private market.

Until recently, Citizens premiums were the highest rate allowed by law. This was to keep Citizens from competing with private insurance companies. Further, insurance agents were not allowed to write policies through Citizens if there was a private carrier who could write the policy.

However, the law has recently changed and Citizens is charging lower premiums and, if they can write a comparable policy for less, the agent does not have to use the private insurance carrier.

CHAPTER 11

Florida Residency For Tuition Purposes

It pays to be a Florida resident student. Literally. In-state tuition at a Florida public university or community college can save a student thousands of dollars in obtaining a degree. Additionally, students who wish to qualify for state financial aid programs such as Bright Futures must be Florida residents.

Florida residence for tuition purposes is not the same as being a Florida resident for other purposes. It takes more than just intent.

Section 1009.21 of the Florida Statutes outlines the requirements for establishing Florida residency for tuition purposes. The specific requirements are contained in rules adopted by the State Board of Education and the Board of Governors for the State University System.

To qualify as a Florida resident for tuition purposes, the student must be a U.S. citizen or lawful permanent resident, and must have established physical and legal residence in Florida for at least 12 months prior to the first day of classes.

Living in or attending school in Florida will not, by itself, establish legal residence for tuition purposes. The 12 month qualifying period must be for the purpose of maintaining a bonafide domicile. The student who comes to Florida to enroll full-time in a Florida school as an out-of-state resident and continuously enrolls in a Florida school will not normally meet the residency requirement. The student must be able to show that her presence and activities in Florida during the 12 month period are not primarily student related.

Students who depend on out-of-state parents for financial support ("Dependent Students") are presumed to be residents of the same state as their parents. These students usually cannot be Florida residents for tuition purposes. However, if the student who depends on her out-of-state parents for support has lived in Florida for 5 consecutive years prior to enrolling at a Florida college, she may be able to qualify as a Florida resident for tuition purposes.

The statute provides certain circumstances to try to clarify its intent.

1. If the parents of a Dependent Student are divorced, the student will be considered a Florida resident for tuition purposes if one of the parents is a Florida resident. This is true even if the student depends on the out-of-state parent for support.

2. If you are a Florida resident, marrying someone who is an out-of-state resident won't disqualify you. However, you will not automatically qualify for Florida residency based solely on a marriage to a Florida resident.

3. A student cannot lose his status as a Florida resident solely by reason of his service or his parent's service in the Armed Forces outside of Florida.

4. If a dependent student loses her resident tuition status because her parents became residents of another state, the student will have a 12-month grace period to receive the benefits of in-state tuition.

Even if you do not meet the 12 month requirement, you still may qualify for an exception. You may be able to be classified as a "temporary resident" for tuition purposes. These exceptions are:

1. Dependent children residing continuously for at least 5 years with an adult relative other than the parent who is a Florida resident.

2. Persons married to legal Florida residents and who intend to make Florida their permanent home and who relinquish all legal ties to any other state. This means they cannot have an out-of-state drivers license or voter registration.

3. Persons who were enrolled as Florida residents for tuition purposes at a Florida public college, but who abandon Florida residency, can re-enroll in Florida within 12 months of the abandonment provided she continuously maintains her Florida residency while enrolled. This exception can only be used one time.

4. Active duty members of the United State Armed Services or Florida National Guard residing or stationed in Florida. Also, an active duty member of the U.S. Armed Services stationed outside of Florida and the spouses and dependent children can attend a public Florida college located within 50 miles of the military establishment where they are stationed, if the

military establishment is located within a county bordering Florida.

5. Full time teachers and administrators of the State of Florida public school system.

A full list of the exceptions can be found in Section 1009.21 of the Florida Statutes.

Residency Documentation. In order to prove your qualification for Florida residency for tuition purposes, many Florida schools require supporting documentation. Not every institution requires the same materials. Below is a brief list of examples.

1. Documentation establishing legal residence in Florida:
   - proof of maintaining one-year of residency (deed to a home or, if you are renting, rent receipts, cancelled checks or notarized statement from a landlord).

2. Documentation to show that residence is permanent and not just for the purpose of or incidental to enrollment in school.
   - voter registration card,
   - drivers license,
   - vehicle registration, and
   - employment verification

3. Many schools will also look for other documents or factors that support the student's intent to make Florida a permanent home.

Of course, there should not be any contrary evidence which shows the student has established or maintained a residence outside of Florida.

CHAPTER 12

Boating And Fishing In Florida

REGISTERING A BOAT IN FLORIDA. Florida is a boater's paradise. It has miles and miles of coastline, boater friendly waterways and restaurants and resorts that are accessible only by boat.

The purchaser of a new boat has 30 days to apply for registration and title. This application must be made at the county tax collector's office, either in the county where the boat is located or where the boat owner resides.

During the 30 day grace period, you must keep a copy of the bill of sale with proof of the date of purchase aboard the vessel. If you operate an unregistered vessel after 30 days, you can be charged with a second degree misdemeanor.

To register and title your boat (both are required), you must complete Form HSMV 82040 and submit it, along with the Manufacturer's Statement of Origin (or its equivalent) and the registration fee and titling fee to the county tax collector's office.

Out-Of-State Vessels. For snowbirds bringing their boat to Florida, the state recognizes valid registration certificates and numbers issued to visiting boaters for a period of 90 days. If you intend to use your boat in Florida for longer than 90 days, you must register it with a county tax collector. You may retain your out-of-state registration number if you plan to bring the boat back to your home state within a reasonable period of time.

Exemptions. Certain vessels are exempt from registration or titling, or both. Boats without motors, boats used exclusively on private lakes and ponds, vessels owned by the U.S. government, and boats used strictly as lifeboats for other boats do not require registration.

A boat is exempt form titling if it falls under one of these categories:

- boats without motors that are less than 16 feet in length,
- vessels used strictly in private lakes and ponds,
- vessels owned by the U.S. government or State of Florida, and
- vessels already registered in another state (subject to the 90 day restriction mentioned above).

Transferring Title. If, after moving to Florida, you purchase a previously owned boat, you must have the title transferred into your name and you must register the boat.

At the time of purchase, the seller must deliver to you a valid certificate of title with an assignment on it showing transfer of the title to your name. You then have 30 days to file an application for a title transfer with the county tax collector.

Registration Number and Decal. Each registered vessel in Florida receives a registration number. This number is permanent and remains with the vessel as long as it is operated or stored in Florida, even if ownership changes.

The registration number must be painted or permanently attached to both sides of the bow (the front half of the boat for you landlubbers) and must be in block letters and numerals at least 3 inches in height. The number consists of a prefix of letters (i.e. FL), a set of numerals and a suffix of letters. When you apply the registration number you must separate the prefix and suffix from the numbers with a space equal to the width of a digit. The number should read as follows: FL 1234 AB. The registration number must read from left to right, must contrast in color with the hull and must be maintained in a legible condition.

Each year that you register the boat, you'll receive a decal signifying the year during which the registration is valid. You must display this decal on the port (left) side of the vessel, either immediately before or after the registration number. You must remove the previous year's decal.

Registration Renewal. If you own your boat in your individual name, the registration period begins on the first day of your birth month and ends the last day of the month immediately preceding your birth month in the next year.

If you co-own the boat with others, the registration period will be based on the birthday of the person whose name first appears on the registration. You must renew the registration each year within the 30 day period ending at midnight on the owner's date of birth.

For vessels owned by companies, corporations or dealers, the registration period begins July 1 and ends June 30 of the next year. The renewal period is the 30 day period beginning June 1.

FLORIDA FISHING LICENSE. Florida means fishing. Florida boasts some of the best saltwater and freshwater fishing anywhere. The center of the state has a multitude of freshwater lakes and ponds. The Florida Keys are renowned for their sport fishing and Boca Grande on the Gulf Coast is regarded as the home of the world's greatest tarpon fishing.

Florida requires most of its recreational anglers to obtain a fishing license. While this applies to both residents and non-residents, Florida residents have the unique option of purchasing lifetime licenses.

Licensing for fishing is governed by the Florida Fish and Wildlife Conservation Commission (FWC). The FWC offers those with a major credit card the choice of purchasing a fishing license from home by telephone or the internet. You can call 1-888-FISH-FLORIDA (347-4356) or visit http://myfwc.com and follow the instructions. Either way, you will obtain a temporary license number immediately so you can fish right then. The FWC will mail your permanent license to you within 48 hours.

You may also obtain your license from any county tax collector's office or certain authorized sporting goods stores or fishing retailers.

Types of Licenses. Depending on your interests and your budget, you have several choices of licenses if you are a Florida resident. Freshwater fishing licenses and saltwater fishing licenses are available in one or five year terms. Residents can also purchase one-year combination licenses such as freshwater/saltwater fishing combo, freshwater fishing/hunting combo and freshwater/saltwater fishing/hunting combo.

Nonresident freshwater fishing licenses and saltwater fishing licenses are available in 3-day, 7-day, and 1-year increments and are considerably more expensive than resident's licenses.

In addition to your saltwater fishing license, if you are fishing for snook, lobster or tarpon, you must purchase a permit for each.

Florida Residency for Fishing Purposes. In order to qualify as a Florida resident for the purpose of purchasing a fishing license, you must have resided in Florida for 6 continuous months prior to the issuance and you must either claim Florida as your primary residence or be a member of the U.S. Armed Forces Stationed in Florida.

Freshwater Exemptions. You do not need a freshwater fishing license if you are:

- a child under 16 years of age.
- a resident who is a member of the U.S. Armed Forces.
- fishing in your county of residence on our homestead or homestead of your spouse or minor child.
- a person fishing in a fish pond of 20 acres or less which is located entirely within private property and is not connected to public waters.
- a resident fishing with live or natural bait using a pole or line not equipped with a reel (cane pole).
- a resident 65 years of age or older who has in his possession proof of age and residency (drivers' license).

- a resident who is certified as totally and permanently disabled.

Saltwater Exemptions.   You do not need a saltwater fishing license if you are:

- a child under 16 years of age.
- a resident who is a member of the U.S Armed Forces.
- a resident fishing in saltwater from land or from a structure fixed to land.
- a person fishing in saltwater from a for-hire vessel (charter boat) that has a valid vessel license.
- a resident 65 years of age or older who has in his possession proof of age and residency (drivers' license).

ABOUT THE AUTHOR

Dean Hanewinckel, an attorney in Englewood, Florida, has helped his clients meet their legal needs since 1984. He is the founder of the Law Offices of Dean Hanewinckel, P.A., a law firm representing and counseling clients in the areas of estate planning, real estate law and business law.

He has written numerous published articles on these subjects. Many of these articles can be found on his website at www.dean-law.com, where you can also get information about planning an estate when you move to Florida.

He was born in New Orleans, Louisiana, and earned his business and law degrees from the University of Florida. He is a member of the Real Property, Probate and Trust Law Section of the Florida Bar, the Charlotte County and Sarasota County Bar Associations and was a past member of the National Association of Bond Lawyers. Dean has served on a number of boards of charitable organizations in his community.

FURTHER RESOURCES

Additional information, including articles, links to helpful government and informational sites on the internet, and forms, can be found at www.newfloridaresident.com.

CPSIA information can be obtained
at www.ICGtesting.com
Printed in the USA
BVOW11s0204010917

493549BV00008B/164/P